House of Faith or Enchanted Forest?

House of Faith or Enchanted Forest?

American Popular Belief in an Age of Reason

CHARLES W. HEDRICK

CASCADE *Books* · Eugene, Oregon

HOUSE OF FAITH OR ENCHANTED FOREST?
American Popular Belief in an Age of Reason

Cascade Books
A Division of Wipf and Stock Publishers
199 W. 8th Ave., Suite 3
Eugene, OR 97401

www.wipfandstock.com

ISBN 13: 978-1-60608-006-1

Cataloging in Publication data:

Hedrick, Charles W.
    House of faith or enchanted forest? : American popular belief in an age of reason /
Charles W. Hedrick.

    xviii + 98 p. ; 23 cm. Includes bibliography.

    ISBN 13: 978-1-60608-006-1

    1. United States—Religion. 2. Religion and culture—United States. I. Title.

BL2525 H40 2009

Manufactured in the U.S.A.

In memory of *Peter Abelard (1079–1142),
and, in particular, his *Sic et Non* (Yes and No), where he set
before his students pros and cons of contradictory positions on
Christian faith and encouraged his students to rely on their
own reason in critically examining the sources.

"The first key of wisdom is called assiduous and frequent questioning . . ."

—Peter Abelard, *Sic et Non*[1]

1. Polka and Bernard, *Readings in Western Civilization*, vol. 1, 114.

CONTENTS

PREFACE

This book, written by one who made his living as an academic, is for the general public not the Academy. It consists of brief essays challenging popularly held religious beliefs current in America at the beginning of the twenty-first century. Each essay is directly addressed to the reader and framed as one side of a public dialogue about private personal faith and values. Most were written over a twenty-year period (1986–2006) and published as Religion and Ethics editorials in the *Springfield News-Leader* (daily newspaper in Springfield, Missouri, owned by Gannett Co., Inc.). The circulation of this newspaper, Monday through Friday, is approximately 60,400 and Sunday 87,300; the Religion and Ethics editorial usually appeared weekly on Wednesday.

I was ordained to the ministry by the First Baptist Church of Greenville, Mississippi, on July 8, 1956. I served as pastor of Baptist churches in Mississippi and California for seven years and a Congregationalist church in New York City for one year. I was commissioned as an Army Reserve chaplain on September 8, 1964, and retired on April 30, 1994, with the rank of Colonel after thirty-three years of service. After teaching in the Department of Religious studies for twenty-four years at Missouri State University, I retired as Distinguished Professor Emeritus.

The essays were written deliberately for a popular audience. I have always thought of the newspaper as a public forum, and the essays were a way of bringing the community at large into an academic classroom. My goal was provoking thought on issues a thoughtful person might inevitably ponder in private moments. We are most nearly honest with ourselves in the privacy of our own heads. In any case, persons educated in the American public school system, which for the most part is secular, can scarcely avoid the challenge reason presents to traditional religious faith.

There was also a subversive reason for choosing a public forum. I wanted to get around the religious professionals, who control thinking about religion and values in America from their "bully pulpits." I chose a public venue to avoid using the technical jargon of an academic publication, which is not read by the public in any case. Academics write "scholar-speak," meaning that they observe certain literary conventions expected in the academic study of religion. Sometimes it can be dry as a bone and at others absolutely scintillating—if the reader knows the dialect. Religious professionals, on the other hand, speak "religionese," meaning that they are required to observe "the language of Zion," as spoken and written in their communities of faith. Both idioms, for different reasons, are barriers to general readers hoping for plain-spoken candor. In writing this book I have aimed at candor in the vernacular, the language of the street.

The newspaper is the only inexpensive forum offering an opportunity for widespread engagement with a popular audience. I intended that each editorial raise public awareness about significant issues of faith and values in twentieth—and now twenty-first-century—America. The church and synagogue will not normally raise such issues because the very raising of them tends to undermine the institution of public religion—and also because the church and synagogue cannot satisfactorily resolve them. Such issues are raised in the academy as a matter of course, but the audience is miniscule.

Springfield, Missouri, might be described as a "buckle on the Bible belt" (one of many in the country, no doubt). Springfield is the third largest city in the state and is most accurately described as a religiously conservative "church town." The International Headquarters of both the Assemblies of God and the Baptist Bible Fellowship are located here. The Assemblies have a theological seminary in the city, as well as two colleges (Central Bible College and Evangel University), and the Baptist Bible Fellowship has one college (Baptist Bible College). A Southern Baptist College can be found at nearby Bolivar, Missouri (Southwest Baptist University). Drury University, also located in Springfield, has distant connections with the

Christian Church tradition. The payrolls of these institutions constitute a significant economic influence on the city and surrounding region.

To judge from responses to the editorials printed in the letters to the editor, the religious right found the essays challenging, since they were forced to consider inconsistencies in the traditional Judeo-Christian religious worldview. Even thoughtful people from the left had difficulty with them. One good friend, a minister at a progressive church in Springfield, once told me that I should write something "relevant" for the newspaper. And when the editorial page editor for the *News-Leader* changed in 2006 my columns were ruled "irrelevant" because they don't "tie into any issue going on in the world." I leave that for readers to decide.

My thanks are due to JoAnne Brown, James A. Kellett, and Morey McDaniel. They read the manuscript when it was nearly completed and suggested improvements. I am grateful for their suggestions, some accepted and others not, but in no way should the reader hold them responsible for the finished product.

INTRODUCTION

The House of Faith

Until the latter half of the twentieth century, the public face of religion in America was conceived as Judeo-Christian, represented by three religious groups. The largest were Roman Catholic and *Protestant. Judaism was much smaller. That these three religious bodies are institutionalized in the public psyche as "American religion" is due largely to our European roots. We inherited these religious groups from Europe in the various waves of immigration through our history. As a case in point, the United States military, since World War II and until recently, only endorsed chaplains for military services from these bodies.[1]

The Roman Catholic Church represents a single monarchical community with unified religious beliefs and practices, controlled by a religious leader who speaks for God in matters of religion. People of Jewish faith consist of four segments: *Orthodox, Conservative, Reformed, and Reconstructionist, and while these four bodies form four distinct approaches to Judaism, they are clearly part of one religion. Thus chaplains from any of these three Jewish bodies were designated simply "Jewish" by the armed services.

Under the Protestant rubric, however, were crammed an assortment of religious groups quite diverse in ideology, praxis, and faith, having little specific connection to one another, except that their origins were inspired by the same Judeo-Christian tradition, brought to America by the churches coming out of the *Protestant Reformation. For example, the Church of Jesus Christ of Latter-day Saints (Mormons), founded in 1830 as an indigenous American religion, is regarded as a branch of Protestantism for the purpose of endorsing chaplains for the military. Even Native Americans, for the purpose of chaplain's coverage, were grouped under the Protestant rubric. Roman Catholic and Jewish chaplains are responsible for religious ministry to the people of their faiths and Protestant chaplains, regardless of their own denomination, theoretically serve everyone else. I must quickly add, however, that chaplains, regardless of their own faith, are responsible to ensure that the religious needs of all faiths in their military units are met.

All three of these bodies (Protestant, Catholic, and Jewish) are historically related, and all three, in part, use the same set of holy texts, the Hebrew Bible—Jews call this collection of texts the Jewish Scriptures, or Torah, while Roman Catholics and Protestants dub them the "Old Testament." Hence, Roman Catholics and Protestant groups are *Judeo* in the sense that they, in part (and the larger part at that!), use the Jewish Scriptures. Jews and Protestants have the same books in Torah/Old Testament, while Roman Catholics use several other texts referred to as *deutero-canonical, meaning they were added to the *canon at a later time, but nevertheless are just as authoritative as the *proto-canonical books used by Jews and Christians. Roman Catholics and Protestants in America also use the same collection of New Testament texts.

Only in recent memory have religious groups, completely unrelated to the historical circumstances that brought floods of European immigrants to the New World, become competing religious forces in America. Within the last twelve years, for example, the U.S. military has integrated Islamic and *Buddhist chaplains into the military services along with the traditional categories of Jewish, Catholic, and Protestant.

Because these three religious bodies share religious texts and have a historical connection, they share a similar complex of religious ideas and practices; these ideas still form the backbone of American religion— especially in its popular form. Only in 2007, has someone of non Judeo-Christian faith been elected to national office: Rep. Keith Ellison, a

*Muslim (Democrat from Minnesota), was sworn into the U. S. House of Representatives using the *Qur'an the sacred writings of Islam! Nevertheless, the religious face of America at this point still remains predominately Judeo-Christian.[2]

This book addresses the complex of traditional Jewish and Christian ideas and ethical values shared by Jewish, Protestant, and Catholic groups, since the founding of this country. Because of the dominant influence of the Judeo-Christian faith in American culture, many of these same basic ideas are shared by the general public, although they may have only a peripheral association with church or synagogue; these views are also shared, at least in part, by those who have abandoned involvement in the traditional worship of synagogue and church.[3]

Here is one example of grassroots popular belief. In 1986, the Southern Baptist Convention appointed a Peace Committee to bring about harmony between the warring factions of the Southern Baptist Convention. They wrote:

> We, as a Peace Committee, have found that most Southern Baptists [believe that the Bible has] 'truth without any mixture of error for its matter,' . . . meaning . . . that:
>
> (1) They believe in direct creation of mankind and therefore they believe that Adam and Eve were real persons.
>
> (2) They believe that the named authors did indeed write the biblical books attributed to them by those books.
>
> (3) They believe the miracles described in Scripture did indeed occur as supernatural events in history.
>
> (4) They believe that the historical narratives given by biblical authors are indeed accurate and reliable as given by those authors.[4]

These specific religious views, with some modification here and there, are generally shared by a majority of people in America having religious roots in the Judeo-Christian tradition.[5]

Although the probes of the essays were gentle and some slightly tongue-in-cheek, the issues they raise for traditional faith are anything but harmless. For reflective souls, heirs of the *Renaissance and *Enlightenment, trying to make modern sense of ancient religions in the twenty-first century, the essays raise disturbing questions that the church and synagogue have never resolved and, likely, never will.

The Enchanted Forest: An Allegory

In general people don't take the time to reflect on the religious ideas picked up from parents, taught to them in church and synagogue by religious professionals, learned in school from religious teachers, or picked up from American culture (calendared holy days, TV, newspaper, etc.). These ideas, basically Judeo-Christian in origin, are simply accepted as religious cultural bedrock by the general public. Seldom is the worldview they represent viewed as a whole. Usually such ideas are encountered piecemeal in confessions, creeds, or as isolated ideas from the Bible. So, of course, God created the world—it's in the Bible! Of course God answers prayer! Of course we are all sinners, because Adam and Eve sinned in the Garden of *Eden! What follows is an attempt to show how these ideas appear when they are presented in a package. Popular religion in these United States appears very much like an enchanted forest:

Once upon a time a Utopian garden existed in an enchanted wood. Except for a deceitful talking serpent the couple living there dwelled in perfect harmony with both plant and animal life and had all their needs provided. Rules existed in the garden: no eating the fruit of a certain tree; it would destroy the couple's innocence. The couple broke the rule, were forced out of the garden into an enchanted forest where life was hard. But that was long ago; today no one recalls the exact location of the garden.

In those olden days, delightful creatures, *unicorns (Psalm 22:21) and humanoid cherubs having four faces (Ezekiel 1:5–6) roamed the enchanted forest, along with monsters, like dragons and the frightful monster of the deep, Leviathan (Psalm 74:13–14). Although dinosaurs never existed in the forest, horrid demons lurked there: satyrs (Leviticus 17:7), the night demon Lilith (Isaiah 34:14), and the "noonday devil" (Psalm 91:6). In modern times, predatory demons still prowl the forest, seeking to do evil to the inhabitants or causing them to behave wickedly. But angelic creatures in the en-

chanted forest protect them from demonic evil and other disasters. Some dangers in the forest threatening to human life, however, seem worse than the demons—disastrous floods, tornados, hurricanes, diseases, and the like. Yet, the inhabitants say, everything in the forest always works out for the best in spite of these terrible events.

The economy of the forest is minutely managed by an all-powerful benevolent designer, who fashioned the forest to precise specifications and routinely runs it like clockwork according to a master plan. Although the designer is never seen anywhere, he nevertheless is accessible at all times to everyone who speaks to him. He takes requests, and sometimes is thought to cure diseases. Most people are greatly comforted by speaking to him, although he never answers directly.

The designer manages the inhabitants of the forest through guardians who interpret the rules for all inhabitants. The first rule in the forest is required attendance at weekly group meetings, during which the guardians explain how life in the forest is to be lived; rule two requires exact compliance with all the minutiae of rule one. If these two rules are followed, the irregularities sometimes disrupting the harmony of the forest will not occur. The designer uses disasters to get the inhabitants' attention when they forget rules one and two.

All worthwhile knowledge is found in a Book written long ago by the designer himself. The guardians are the chief interpreters of the Book, since the inhabitants long ago gave up being concerned with the ancient past and the designer languages in which the Book was written. Today, however, few even of the guardians bother with the ancient languages; they simply assume modern translations of the Book are invested with the designer's authority. Among other things, the Book describes our past, present, and future. Apparently being captivated by the view of life in the enchanted forest is preparation for admission to the Utopian garden where it all began. Although no one knows where the garden is, most anyone living in the forest will confidently tell any traveler how to get there.

My point is this: the truths we live by are like one-eyed angels who see only in single dimensions.

This brief allegory, a thinly disguised caricature, reflects the general views of Judeo-Christian religion in America today. The following essays address aspects of America's enchanted forest, but only in an indirect and conversational way.

1. GOD IN THE AMERICAN STREETS

Belief in the existence of God remains constant in American culture. For most Americans, God, however conceived, is creator of all and has endowed the universe with balance and regularity. For religious people, balance and regularity in the universe lead to the idea of a designing "intelligence" behind the universe. Even those who are not particularly religious would likely agree, because they share the traditional view that God created the universe. After all, things had to begin somewhere—so the popular rationale would go. Unfortunately, disturbing events in the modern world raise questions about the idea of a "Designer." For example, *What is the "intelligence" in intelligent design?*

Clearly the universe has regularity; yet things do not always work exactly the same. For example, light sometimes acts like waves and sometimes like particles, the scientists tell us. Most physicists recognize both regularity and randomness in the universe. But to describe its regularity as the "design" of a particular "intelligence" is essentially a confessional, not a scientific, statement. The "confession" derives in part from observable reality, and in part from religious ideas, and it is not the only way to account for the universe. A religious physicist, working with strict standards for scientific statements, might make a religious "confession" about the origins of the universe but would not pass it off as scientific—unless he or she had a particular agenda.

"Designs" are not always deliberate or intelligent. For example, anyone who has ever made an ink blot knows that the particular design one achieves is not deliberate but only accidental, produced by the amount and consistency of the ink and the way pressure is applied—a purely fortuitous product, it would seem. Cancers also have design—but what kind of intelligence would deliberately design a cancer into the fabric of the universe?

The idea that our universe is, more or less, regular does not lead inevitably, or even necessarily, to an intelligent designer—and certainly not to a benign intelligence. Some could well conclude that the intelligence behind the universe is careless, capricious—or worse, devious. What sort of intelligence would design a universe purposely hostile to life? Yet we seem to have such a universe. Debilitating disease (cancer, birth defects, cerebral palsy, arthritis, Alzheimer's, etc.) and natural "acts of God" (like tornados, hurricanes, and floods) are apparently designed into our present universe.

In antiquity, some groups opposed the idea that a benevolent God fashioned the universe. Mindful of the suffering in the world, they argued that the fashioner was flawed, stupid, or even evil. How could caring intelligence deliberately produce a universe so frightfully hostile to humanity? Christians and Jews argued back that the designer did not originally create such a world. God created a world suitable for, and beneficial to, humankind (Genesis 1:31). As a result of willful creaturely rebellion, however, the designer then deliberately "cursed" the world to punish humanity (Genesis 3:17–19). But this does not solve the problem, for, like it or not, the "designer" is still left with responsibility for our hostile world. Cursing a world hospitable to human life over one infraction hardly seems the act of a caring intelligence. In arguing "intelligent design" the problem is how to distance the designer from the present world.

Could one also surmise that the designer simply abandoned the universe? Possibly, and without the designer's oversight, creatures abandoned in a hostile world must adapt or perish, and, that seems to be the situation in which we find ourselves. In this world, as presently ordered, we either adapt or perish—as Mr. *Darwin argued nearly 150 years ago.

⊰◈⊱

We usually describe God in terms of the attributes with which we endow him.[1] For instance, he gets angry with sin (wrath), he punishes the evildoer (retribution), he loves his creatures, he is patient, he forgives (merciful), etc. We don't reflect on God as an entity with "personhood," but rather only in terms of how we think God reacts to us. We don't think God is a blind force, but rather as a deliberative deity who reflects the very best of our own human characteristics. At least we use our best features to describe him, so it is surprising we don't inquire into God's mind, and ask questions like *does God ever muse about things?*

What does God think about when he has time on his hands (so to speak)? Is God introspective or curious? Does he ever daydream? Has he ever had a new thought—an "Aha" experience? The question is not far fetched, since the Bible portrays God in the first account of creation giving himself a reflective pat on the back ("he saw that it was good," Genesis 1:4, 10, 12, 18, 21, 25, 31), and kicking back for a rest on the seventh day (Genesis 2:2). In a second account of creation, he takes time off for a relaxing walk in *Eden "in the cool of the day" (Genesis 3:8)—still the custom in the modern Mediterranean world. I know some will object: "metaphors"! These are just figures of speech—the biblical writer is not speaking literally. Still, even to use such images begs the question: does God ever take time off from the business of running the world, curing disease, punishing the wicked, and the like, or is his divine mind always occupied with the cosmos and its creatures?

Does it really matter? Well, perhaps not to you, but it mattered a great deal to some of the ancient philosophers. For them, the ideal state for a God was "at rest." God existed in silence, singularity, solitariness, and stillness—he even moved "motionlessly"! Movement, or thought, changed the deity, and change was a flaw. Deity, as they conceived it, was truly the same yesterday, today, and forever—without beginning, without end.

On the other hand, the popular view in ancient Mediterranean culture conceived of the Gods actively involving themselves in human affairs—destroying and protecting cities, devising plagues, working miraculous cures, discoursing with human beings, and much more. Today God is conceived more like the ancient popular view than the philosophical view. God is constant motion 24/7, everywhere at the same instant, juggling myriads of activities, starting plagues, performing miraculous cures, creating hurricanes, answering prayers, winning ball games—to mention just a few.

The philosophers would say about my curiosity, "what a nerdy question. Of course God does not dream, because his dreams, like his words, would be divine 'things' existing apart from him, and his former singularity would devolve into a duality—or worse." They thought of God as an irreducible singular entity—a *Monad.

Today in western culture, we also think of God as Monad—on our best days we are not *polytheistic. On the other hand, Christianity is mostly *Trinitarian—the affirmation of three distinct persona in one Godhead. This concept would strike the ancient philosophers as theoretically improbable because it employs plurality to explain God's nature.

I prefer to think of God as sentient—a thinking being. And if God thinks, he is apt to be curious, think new thoughts, and even daydream. The philosophers would rightly object: if so, he is not "the same yesterday, today, and forever." Others might object that I am simply inventing God in my own image! Perhaps so, but doesn't everybody?

❦

During droughts in the American Midwest believers of all stripes will turn to God petitioning for rain for the crops. Indeed, petitioning God for a variety of things we humans find necessary for life is pretty much general practice in America. We seem to think that God, however we conceive him, is interested in the minutiae of each human life. It does not matter whether a person regularly and formally prays or not about such matters, in the streets people generally assume that God does control nature and natural occurrences. But certain events do seem to challenge such an idea.

The wake of destruction and death left by the *tsunami in Indonesia in 2004 and category-four hurricane Katrina in 2005 beg the question: who controls the weather, God or Mother Nature? The Bible does not portray *Yahweh, God of Jewish and Christian faith, directly administering the day-to-day routine of nature, as ancient nature Gods are portrayed. The regularity of their cult rituals was believed to ensure both the benevolence of the natural processes and the fertility of fields and flocks—though not even they were always able to control the weather (1 Kings 18:17–29). The *Canaanite God *Ba'al, for example, was portrayed as the God of storms. Ruling over wind and clouds, his power was manifested in thunder and lightening. Yahweh, on the other hand, "earned his spurs" and made his reputation controlling history (Exodus 4:22–23; 15:21) and managing the religious welfare of the Israelites. He was far more interested in their religious obedience than directly maintaining the harmony and rhythm of the natural order. Rather than ensuring annual harvests by day-to-day hands-on (so to speak) management of nature, Yahweh is portrayed managing people by using nature to reward obedience and punish disobedience (Deuteronomy 28:1–46). Thus it seems more proper to say: Yahweh used nature when it served his purpose, but he is not generally portrayed directly juggling the daily routine of the physical elements, which was the nature God's primary concern.

Whether Yahweh used nature wisely, or morally, however, is an open question. For example, he is portrayed as authorizing the killing of Job's children (with a great wind, Job 1:19) as part of a bargain with Satan (1:9–12). Because of human "wickedness" (Genesis 6:5), he flooded the earth, obliterating every living thing (Genesis 6:17)—he thought better of it later, however (Genesis 8:21; 9:11). He destroyed the cities of Sodom and Gomorrah and everyone in them by means of fire and brimstone (Genesis 19:24–25—was it a volcanic eruption?), and he was also known to use hurricanes (Psalm 83:13–15). Hence, it appears that his periodic use of nature in the Bible is consistent with the recent tragedies in Indonesia and the Gulf.

Apparently God can control weather when he chooses, but he seems less inclined to regulate nature directly day by day, preferring to manipulate it from time to time for reasons known only to him. When we do know his reasons for interfering in the natural processes, he seems (from our perspective) to be a bit heavy-handed. The biblical record raises two questions: does God actually govern nature in a hands-on way (so to speak), or has he set an unregulated system in place, leaving to "Mother Nature" its day-to-day operation, which he manipulates from time to time? The more serious question is this: is it moral to use weather to reward and punish? Even we morally-challenged humans know degrees of evil exist in the world, and justice demands that they draw different degrees of punishment appropriate to the crime. But no such discrimination exists in "natural" disasters. The innocent suffer along with the guilty. If God uses storms to punish evildoers—such as using Katrina "to get those damn casinos" (as some suggested)—then in the process he is also taking out hospitals, seminaries, and orphanages! Describing "natural disasters" as "acts of God" makes God look incompetent or immoral; it seems best to chalk up such disasters to Mother Nature and revise your personal theology.

⸙

Of course, maybe God has nothing to do with weather at all and the climate of a given region is a natural phenomenon and as such is simply due to luck, a comment that begs the question, *What controls our lives: divine providence or "lady" luck?* At some point everyone has said: "What a great stroke of luck," or "We survived by the providence of God." As a Baptist, I understand "divine providence" but what is "luck" and how do I reconcile it to the dominant idea in western culture that God somehow regulates the universe?

My brother-in-law had a great game of golf one weekend—even for him. He shot 67 for 18 holes including a hole-in-one. His wife chalked up the hole-in-one to his skill with the clubs. But he insisted "No, anytime you shoot a hole-in-one, it's luck." I thought about it for a moment and had to agree. If holes-in-one were due to skill there would be more of them. So I suggested: "Perhaps it was divine providence." He replied: "No, it's luck; God doesn't care about golf." My brother-in-law is a Baptist deacon, so I had to take him seriously. After all, golf is a game where you play against yourself, so the only plausible reason for God to intervene in his game and "bless" him with a hole-in-one was to lower his golf score and make him feel rather smug. We usually like to think God has bigger issues on his plate, which is what I think he meant by "God couldn't care less about golf."

What we seem to mean by "luck" is that sometimes things go in our favor and at other times they do not, including even the most trivial matters. We seem to conceive luck as a pervasive random force in the universe that, for whatever reason, is erratic or whimsical in application. If this is true, we do not live in a universe where *everything* is micromanaged by God. Hence, people who believe in God's providence must cope with the disturbing idea that God manages, or micromanages, some things, but allows other things simply to happen, as they will, without his oversight. Or, on the other hand, we live in a world where God micromanages everything and must be given the credit (or the blame) for *everything* that happens. If God is to get the "credit" for everything that happens, then we humans bear no responsibility for global warming, poverty, the breach in the ozone layer, or the failure of the levees in New Orleans in 2005. Somehow, however, we instinctively know that we cannot make God the "scapegoat" for all the misfortunes of the world. Most of us realize (I hope) that God did not cause the *ENRON debacle, or the incompetent response of the Federal Government to the disaster in New Orleans in the aftermath of Katrina.

Perhaps "luck" is only a more or less natural "force," in the universe— something like gravity, for example. While the ancient Greeks and Romans personified it into a deity named *Tyche, we moderns have secularized it. Nevertheless, the idea that some things just happen for no apparent reason is a disturbing concept for those who must think there is a master plan to the universe. If things happen for no reason, then we have a universe permeated by a principle of randomness that suggests God may guide matters in the universe in most instances, but leaves others to happen without his guidance. Such a possibility raises the question: how can we tell "benevolent concern" from "random event"? Perhaps we cannot.

The Bible is full of bad things perpetrated by the biblical God on basically decent people, although many believers seem willing to accept that sometimes God does bad things even to good people for reasons we cannot understand. Job thought so: "Shall we receive good at the hand of God and not evil"? Maybe we invented the idea of "luck" because such apparently capricious behavior on God's part is simply inconsistent with the idea of a benevolent God. But if we invented "luck," we could have invented God as well.

❧◈❧

It is surely questionable that God is concerned with the minutiae of individual human lives or even the mega problems that plague whole nations. During the Second World War the belt buckles of German soldiers were etched with the following slogan: "God is with us." Of course the allied troops thought the same thing, because they too thought their cause was just. And this clash of claims for God's support in the enterprises of our lives naturally raises the question about the minutiae of our lives. For example, *Does God care about baseball?*

Are we to suppose that God follows baseball and even decides the outcomes of games? I recently saw a player, after throwing the winning pitch in a baseball game, make the sign of the cross, kiss his fingers, and point upward—thanking God for the win. Some believe God really involves himself in the minutiae of life—even numbering hairs on the human head and deciding the deaths of sparrows (Matthew 10:29–30). But with such a complicated universe to run, surely God has concerns more pressing than sparrows, hairs in the drain—and the Cardinals/Royals game. In terms of universal importance, which team wins the pennant seems rather insignificant. Some events clearly have a more "profound" impact on life than others. True, the outcome of a Cardinals/Royals game is more significant than hairs left in the drain this morning, but totally insignificant when compared to the Iraqi war. Some die-hard fans may disagree, but in terms of *significant* impact on human life, baseball games fall completely off the radar screen for everyone, except perhaps those involved in the industry.

It comforts us to think there is a master plan to life. Believing that life is "scripted" helps us cope with tragedy and loss. Life must make sense, and even tragedy must have some meaning in the grand scheme of things—or so we insist. Even the death of a butterfly must have a place in God's "master plan." The alternative, thinking we live in an "unscripted" and arbitrary universe, is a frightening concept. In an arbitrary universe, no master plan exists. What happens—happens! Under those conditions, life's meaning is what each of us makes of the random events that constitute our lives.

I personally do not like this alternative and hope that affairs in my life are part of some benevolent design for the universe. Yet I am a little dubious when someone tells me God spends time counting the hairs in my drain and marking the demise of individual sparrows. Such micromanagement will not work in large organizations—and the universe, if anything, is large. Effective management gives priority to the more significant. In a global crisis, I don't want God worrying about minutiae, like the welfare of my wife's tomato plants. Micromanagement may be why we have natural disasters, like floods, earthquakes, or epidemics. Other disasters, like war for example, are inevitably the result of human contrivance.

One should not too quickly criticize the divine Administrator of the universe, however, since we have only the barest inkling of what's involved in running it. The universe may actually be unlimited, and if so, that is a lot of turf to cover, even for God—or so God suggested to Job

(Job 38–41) when Job bitterly complained that God treated him unfairly. If God is weighing the outcomes of baseball games and neglecting the causes of war, he is likely out of touch with what's really happening in his universe—at least in this small corner of an out-of-the-way galaxy. Surely God can find better things to do with his time than ponder the pennant!

❧◆❧

One major stumbling block to religious belief in the twenty-first century is God's silence on matters we people of faith find perplexing. Most of these issues could easily be resolved if only God would be more open with his counsel and obvious about what he expects of us. For example, *Why doesn't God talk out loud anymore?* Perhaps you have never wondered about that, but once upon a time God spoke in an audible voice—but not today! When he needed a national leader for the Israelites, he called out to Moses from a burning bush: "Tell them," he said, "I Am that I Am sent you" (Exodus 4:14; Deuteronomy 4:33–36; 5:26). And though "the word of the LORD was rare in those days," God spoke to Samuel (1 Samuel 3:1–11). Out of a whirlwind (Job 38:1), he dialogued with Job, but whispered in a "small voice" to Elijah (1 Kings 19:12). He addressed audible speech to Gideon, Noah, Jonah, the prophets, and others. In the New Testament two instances are notable: at the baptism of Jesus an audible voice from Heaven announced: "This is my beloved son" (Matthew 3:17), and the same words again from a cloud at the transfiguration (Mark 9:7). The biblical God was a talker! So, why the deafening silence today? If there was ever a time we needed to hear God's voice in our ears, it is now, but today few claim to hear God's voice (some do, of course, but today people hearing voices from clouds are usually institutionalized).

Religious professionals tell us God speaks today through the Bible—which for some is literally the "Words of God." But written words are not a living voice! Quoting the Bible to solve modern social and moral problems really hasn't worked; proponents on all sides of issues use the Bible to support their different views. At best the "written Word" is generally ambiguous on contemporary social issues and requires extensive rationalizing to make the text fit the *modern* situation (the Bible is, after all, a compilation of *ancient* texts). Religious professionals claim an edge on the rest of us in explaining the Bible, and even if they don't, we defer to them anyway. Apparently we think God has privileged communication with them to which the rest of us are not privy.

We seem to have access to God thirdhand at best: once God spoke for himself, but today we only have memoirs from people we believe communicated with God; and most of the memoirs do not appear to be based on what God himself said audibly. Many religious professionals claim God's spirit leads them to the "correct" explanations of the memoirs. But, alas, the religious professionals tell us conflicting things—and on God's authority too! Imagine how easily our moral dilemmas could be resolved if only God spoke to us on point from a burning bush or a cloud in his own voice about abortion, homosexuality, war in Iraq, and care for the environment. Unfortunately the contested issues that divide Americans today are not directly addressed on point by the ancient texts of the Bible.

Why won't God talk to us any more? Why should he need ancient memoirs and middlemen to communicate? A genuine conundrum for which no definitive answer exists! Some say: (a) God doesn't need to speak; the Bible speaks for him. (b) We are too cynical and secular today to believe God even if he did speak; so he doesn't bother. (c) God has oblique ways to communicate; for example, through his spirit by impressions on the human consciousness (but this could only be the "noise" of our own religious engineering). (d) God never really spoke audibly at all; biblical writers described events mythically (if true, it raises interesting questions about the Bible). Whatever the reason, we apparently live in an age when God's living voice has fallen silent, and we no longer hear "from God's mouth to our ears." It is an age when God is absent, some have said, and we are left to ponder God and what he expects with little direct vocal assistance from him. The problem for us now is: How do we discriminate among the insistent voices of religious professionals filling the vacuum with their "right" answers to our perplexing questions?

❖

Our predicament, however, may only be due to *God's sense of humor.* Growing up Baptist, I never thought God had a sense of humor. God seemed so utterly serious—not a droll bone in his entire divine body (so to speak). And no wonder; having to deal with sin, disease, evil, and such, would tend to sober anyone. It all made sense then that God had no lighter side but was always heavily serious—never a wink or a twinkle in his divine eye. But I have to admit there are things in the Bible about God that strike me humorously. Maybe God does have a sense of humor after all—a sort of dark humor, but certainly not slapstick. Take Adam and Eve in the Garden, for example. God places them there in a state of innocence and tells them "Enjoy! But don't eat the fruit of *that* particular tree." They take the bait and "fall" for the joke. Later God comes looking for them. But they hide from the All-knowing and All-seeing One, who, tongue in divine cheek, plays along, calling out, "Where are you guys?"—as if he didn't already know!

God called Moses to go to Egypt and lead the Israelites out of bondage. After God twisted his arm, Moses agreed, and away he went. On the way, he stopped one night at an inn; God met him there and (oddly) tried to kill him (Exodus 4:24–26). Is this another practical joke? Well, can you imagine God "trying" to do something and not being able to do it? "Ha! Gotcha that time, didn't I Moses? Aw, just kidding around!" One practical joke is still in process. Three modern religions worship the same God: Jews, Christians, and *Muslims. Modern Cairo, a bustling city of over 15 million souls, virtually shuts down on Friday. At one in the afternoon prayer rugs come out and millions of men pray in the streets. Mahmoud Tawfik prays to the same God as Solomon Silberstein, who worships at Saturday Temple in Jerusalem. On Sunday in Springfield, Missouri, Mary Smith's "Our Father" ascends to the same God. Each religion thinks of itself as "God's special people"—to the exclusion of the other two religions, I might add; and their holy books prove their paternity as God's own people.

I hesitate to blame God for this strange situation, but if we believe the faithful of these religions, God produced their holy books, which confirm the privileged status of each religious community. The situation is not unlike the "jokes" on Adam, Eve, and Moses. There has to be a little *George Carlin humor in all three claiming to have exclusive access to the divine ear. Can you imagine the God who parted the "Red Sea," made the sun stand still, and raised the dead not being able to correct the record? The brunt of this particular joke seems to be those who fail to recognize how ephemeral their favorite fundamental dogma really is.

Of course, it is possible God has absolutely no sense of humor, and never does the divine equivalent of winking, or tucking tongue in cheek. But I would like to think that God was never really serious about some

things we credit him with—like Samuel telling King Saul, "God said annihilate the *Amalekites" (1 Samuel 15:1–3), or God telling *Abraham,
"sacrifice your son" (Genesis 22:1–3). It seems perfectly clear that God
was never really serious about that last order, since he stops Abraham
from killing the lad (Genesis 22:12). And a God who is not always serious
could very well have a funny bone (so to speak).

⊰◈⊱

Can humans really trust the Gods always to treat us with integrity, when
on our better days we appear to have a sharper sense of morality than they
do on their worse days? We assume Gods will always act with integrity—
after all, they are divine. We expect immoral behavior from demons, but
not from Gods. The record, however, is flawed. For instance, in *Homer's
epic poem the *Illiad* *Zeus deceived *Agamemnon with a lying dream—to
the hurt and detriment of *Achilles (2:1–35). And even *Yahweh, the God
of the Bible, sent a lying spirit to deceive King Ahab of Israel so he would
be defeated in battle. Later he placed lying spirits in the mouths of all the
prophets of Israel (1 Kings 22:19–23). On another occasion, he sent an
evil spirit to torment King Saul (1 Samuel 16:14–15)—strange behavior
for a God! Such behavior by the Gods recalls Homer's description of Zeus'
father, *Cronus, as the God "of the crooked ways" (*Illiad* 2:205).

Humans believe it is not ethical to deceive or mistreat others. And
that is one reason the "serious misconduct and loss of moral value" of
American soldiers in the *Abu Ghraib prison during the Iraqi war was so
reprehensible. The soldiers were held accountable for their actions, but
apparently Gods can act as they wish—and with impunity! We explain
their occasionally shocking ways by arguing that Gods obviously know
the big picture. Since they are Gods, we assume they must know what
is best for us in the long term. Our human view of things is finite; we
see matters dimly and then only in short term. So we conclude: an event
appearing tragic to us must only be so from our limited perspective, for
surely Gods always act justly. For that reason, we tend to think that our
personal tragedies must somehow be for the best. This solution, however,
leaves honest folk with a nagging ethical question: how can bringing
anyone harm ever be considered "good"? Is it possible that Gods do not
always know best after all, and humans invented that idea to cover divine

misbehavior? Or is it, perhaps, possible that the writers of our religious texts have mistakenly misled us? For example, did Jesus really instruct his disciples to take up the sword (Luke 22:36).

The biblical book of Job is one of the clearest examples of divine misbehavior in the literature. Job simply could not understand why tragedy struck his life. When his "friends" told him that God punished him because of his sins, Job was perplexed. He was willing to admit he was not perfect, but he knew his suffering was not proportionate to the sins he committed. And Job actually was correct: God *permitted* his egregious suffering to see if he would commit a greater sin, as the text makes plain (Job 1–2).

"The ends never justify the means" is clearly an idealistic sentiment, and we humans on our worst days never quite measure up. In cases of expediency, we frequently find our ends justifying our means, like at Abu Ghraib, for example. Nevertheless, when we privilege ends over means, we at least know we are traveling down a lower road. And if we finite humans *sometimes* know the difference between high road and low road, shouldn't Gods *always* know the difference?

⧉

Do all things happen for a reason? If I said that someone survived a car crash with barely a scratch but four others in the car were killed outright, most people, religious or not, would likely observe, "stuff happens for a reason." Behind that observation is the popular religious belief that God micromanages the world. But if I were to ask, Was there some divine reason for a bird dropping poop on my forehead rather than my shoulder this morning, many would think my question silly. Nevertheless, a serious issue lies behind both situations: Is anyone completely in charge of the universe?

One answer is that God micromanages the universe. If so, *everything* happens for a reason. A micromanaging God would scarcely leave anything to chance! This line of reasoning leads inevitably to the conclusion that even bad things (New Orleans comes to mind) are due to God's deliberate management. Hence, since by popular definition God can do no wrong, everything apparently bad must really be good—and that includes even the bird poop on my forehead. A micromanaging God would have had good reason for the bird poop—for under the theory of divine micromanagement, God makes *everything* happen for a reason.

Perhaps God only generally manages the universe and is not responsible for *everything* that happens. Under "general" management some things are divinely manipulated but other things are just allowed to happen as they will. Under this theory the universe has been set up to work in a well regulated way, and God only intrudes now and then for whatever reason that strikes the divine fancy. For the most part, things do seem to work fairly well in our world. The world turns with general regularity and only the occasional glitch (New Orleans and cancer come to mind). This theory raises the question: how can we ever really be sure what is deliberately caused by God, what is part of the regular pulse of the universe, and what is a glitch in the system? The bird poop is well accommodated by this explanation, however: it is just one of those billions of little things that never register on the divine radar scope, or simply are part of the regular pulse of the universe where things happen for no particular reason—like a leaf falling off a tree, or bird droppings. I just happened to look up at the opportune time this morning at the precise moment the bird pooped. Such occurrences are part of the regular design of things: leaves fall off trees, and birds poop all over the place. But under this theory one can never be sure of anything God does or does not do.

It is also possible that God has chosen to be an observer of events in a universe designed to run itself, more or less—or worse, God has gone missing. "How could that be possible? God created the world, so why abandon it?" Good question! But since we cannot even prove that God exists, how could we possibly know whether God is missing? A missing God, however, does make a sort of perverted sense of our human situation, and could account for natural disasters and unconscionable human sufferings (New Orleans, *tsunamis, and cancer come to mind)—in short, for whatever reason no one is minding the store! Bird poop on the forehead makes excellent sense in such a world, however; a God absent for the big things could scarcely be expected to be around for the little things.

Perhaps we have simply misunderstood God's character. If God were a bit devious, it could explain the general regularity of the cosmos and its blessings when things work without the glitches—such as natural disasters, the tragedies of disease, and fatal "accidents." In short, God may be prone to be a bit "impish," so to speak. Certain passages in the Bible seem to support such a theory—at least the early Israelites and Christians must have thought so by some of the ways they portrayed God. The book of Job is a case directly on point. Bird poop on the forehead is precisely the kind of thing one might expect from a mischievous God.

Of course, it is always possible there is no God. The only difference between this possibility and the last is that human tragedy and natural disaster could not be caused by a nonexistent God, but must be the result of randomness in a universe that never had a manager of any sort. We would be alone in a sort of well-regulated universe—except for the occasional glitch. Such a situation accommodates regularity, natural disasters, and bird poop on the forehead.

The five possibilities for explaining bird poop and divine management of the universe boil down to this: do you choose to believe in an uptight micromanager, a lax general manager, a God gone missing, a mischievous deity, or in no God at all? One could choose to ignore human experience (which the Bible is), and fashion a God of one's own choosing. I suspect that is what most of us do!

⟨◇⟩

The issues addressed in this section are provocative enough to raise the more basic question about God having a future, particularly in the light of the numerous Gods worshiped through recorded and un-recorded history. Persons even slightly familiar with the history of religions would be unusual had they not in more reflective moments pondered the question: *Does our God have a future?* I know it sounds like a really dumb question. How could God *not* have a future? If anyone or anything has prospects surely God does! From the perspective of world history, however, the question is obvious, for history is littered with decayed temples dedicated to obsolete Gods whose religious communities did not survive the passage of time. In the Judeo-Christian tradition, and modern popular imagination, all other Gods are "false" or imaginary Gods, created in the minds of ignorant and misguided people. In their heyday, however, these other Gods were powerful and controlled the lives of many people for many years. They were loved, feared, and their grace invoked through prayer just as devoutly as the God of *Abraham, *Isaac, and *Jacob is today. Those who believed in these now obsolete Gods were as convinced in their faith as devout believers of the Judeo-Christian God are today.

Every religion assumes that its God has eternal prospects. But the idea that "our God is eternal" is simply wrongheaded, as history shows. The character and personality of a particular God exist principally in the mind, apart from any existence the God may have as an "objective" reality. For example, the *Protestant God did not exist before the sixteenth century. He was conceived and born along with the *Protestant Reformation. The Roman Catholic God was very different—and still is. God as he exists in the minds of Episcopalians today is essentially different from the God of Protestant *Fundamentalists or Unitarians. The Gods of these groups have different views on required ritual, ethical values, sin, forgiveness, and the future—provided we assume (as each group tells us) their teaching derives ultimately from God. If tomorrow, Fundamentalism (for example) ceased to exist, the God of Fundamentalism also ceases to exist—I mean this: since no group would exist to serve his interests, his rites would no longer be available in the marketplace of religions. To be a force in society he would need to be rediscovered all over again. So it is with all religions and Gods. All Gods share a potential for obsolescence. *Apollo and *Zeus are no longer invoked in the warm language of faith as once they were. Their *oracles are silent. The *Hellenistic Gods, *Mithras and *Dionysus, once possessed the keys to eternal life and graciously bestowed that gift throughout the ancient world. Nevertheless, their altar fires are now cold ashes, their ruined temples are hollow shells, and their rites abandoned. Yet in the day of their popularity, their believers would have been shocked at the idea their God would one day be obsolete.

How answer the question: Does our God have a future? Clearly *belief* in a God has a definite future. If history shows anything, it shows human beings as "incurably religious"—even to the point of superstition. Human beings likely will always have a Greater Power they worship and serve, for too many mysteries exist in the universe and our scientists have been unable to answer them all. Yes "God" has a future—although the God we serve today may well *not* have a future. Only so long as a God has believers will he influence society. Thus a God without temples and worshippers to remember his holy days does not exist—at least not in any practical sense. And this observation raises a more annoying question: Does the demise of even one God foreshadow the eventual demise of all Gods?

2. THE BIBLE IN AMERICAN CULTURE

The role of the Bible in American popular culture is surprising. Even intelligent people with advanced academic training tend to treat it as an iconic object or a talisman of some sort, endowing it with honor and respect not extended to any other literature. How should it be treated? *Is the Bible holy relic or historical text?* The answer, of course, depends on who answers the question, but in general in religious faith the Bible is a collection of ancient books holding some kind of divine authority. Unfortunately the books are not unified in their religious values and ethics. One reason so many different religious views exist under the broad umbrella of Christianity is because the Bible itself contains diverse views—even on basic issues. The dissonance is often so great that modern believers can prove almost anything they want using the Bible as their authority. Is that true? *Can you prove whatever you want from the Bible?*

Apparently so, and the reason is that the Bible is a collection of ancient texts written at different times by different people, and hence each text reflects aspects of the cultural, ethical, and religious values of the periods in which each text was written. It is scarcely a unified collection. A simple comparison of modern Christianity and Judaism shows that the Hebrew Bible/Old Testament can be read in widely different ways. Part of the explanation for some of this diversity lies in the history of the various groups using the Bible and not in the Bible itself. But some differences owe to contrasting ideas held by the biblical writers. For example, Paul's view of slavery in the ancient world could easily open him to criticism by modern Christians. Paul never condemned slavery. He seems simply to have accepted it as a part of his world. He did recognize that freedom was better than slavery, however, and so advised slaves to secure their freedom if they could (1 Corinthians 7:20–24). If they could not do so legally, his best advice was that they should remain as they were and wait for the Lord's return and the end of the world, which Paul thought would happen in his own lifetime (1 Corinthians 7:29-31; 1 Thessalonians 4:13–18). He neither criticized the institution of slavery, nor challenged slavery as unconscionable and "unjust."

The "pastor" (a different writer than Paul wrote the *Pastoral Epistles), on the other hand, appears to think that slavery was established by God for the common good. He admonished all slaves to honor their owners so that God and his teaching might not be defamed (1 Timothy 6:1; Titus 2:9). Christian slaves having Christian owners, on the other hand, were to serve all the more effectively, since their owners were fellow Christians. Christian slaves were admonished not to be disrespectful or presume that the faith they shared with their owners gave them an advantage in the household (1 Timothy 6:2). The "pastor" does not challenge the institution of slavery, but simply accepts it as the way things are and shapes his ethical advice to fit the status quo.

The passive acceptance of slavery reflected in these and other biblical texts apparently led an Alabama State Senator (Charles Davidson) to conclude that slavery was "God's will." In May of 1996 he passed out a speech to the Alabama Senate defending the institution of slavery. Davidson's brand of biblical literalism, taking the biblical writers' passive acceptance for advocacy, ignores the Bible's connection to its own past and encourages people to read it as a prescription for the present. We should all be alerted to the Bible's potential for misuse when an elected official makes an argument associating slavery with God's will rather than human depravity, and justifies it by appealing to the Bible.

Perhaps it is time that churches and synagogues (the primary and regular users of the Bible in society) re-evaluate how their members are taught to read and appreciate the Bible. Surely we can insist that our leaders are better informed readers of the Bible and more judicious in its use than Senator Davidson. The senator clearly learned one lesson well: to honor the Bible as "God's Holy Word." It is tragic, however, that no one ever taught him that the biblical texts initially were dialogues with ancient culture. To appreciate their arguments we need to know their cultural context, and the history of the biblical texts as a collection.

⊲◇⊳

The stories of origins in the biblical book of Genesis render, perhaps, the most basic religious narrative in the popular Jewish and Christian mind: the stories of Adam and Eve. They, at once, answer questions about the origin of all things and the presence of evil in the world. But seen from a slightly different perspective the stories resonate differently. Some in antiquity viewed the fall from *Eden as an "escape."

Many people take the (second) account of creation (Genesis 2:4b—3:24; the first account is Genesis 1:1—2:4a) to be literally true: Adam and Eve were the first humans on this planet. Let's grant that for the sake of this brief discussion. The traditional interpretation of Genesis focuses on humankind's loss of innocence and companionship with God. Through the willful disobedience of Adam and Eve, humankind "fell" from Eden and lost *paradise. And so we humans are all sinners by virtue of Adam's lapse and loss of innocence (so the New Testament writer Paul says, Romans 5:12). Another branch of early Christians, however, thought differently. For these other Christians (dubbed *Gnostics in some cases by their opponents), Genesis was a story about the tyranny of a flawed God who was deliberately trying to subject humankind to a life of ignorance. For them, eating the forbidden fruit of the tree of the knowledge was a good thing. In effect, eating the fruit and acquiring knowledge liberated humankind from Eden and the tyranny of a God who was, in the view of these other Christians, much less than ideal.

Under both interpretations, had nothing happened the state of things in the Garden of Eden would remain the same; there would be no progress, no growth, no wickedness, no moral triumph, but only an eternal sameness. Adam and Eve would exist forever in a persistent state of childlike innocence. But for their acquiring knowledge, Adam and Eve would be there still, only the two of them, whiling away the hours with nothing much to do. (Children came after the fall [Genesis 3:16], so presumably no sexual activity could happen in a state of Eden innocence.) True, if there had been no "fall," humankind would have been spared murders, gas chambers, disease, pollution, wars, etc. But, on the other hand, humankind would have lost the excitement of discovery, human achievement, art, music, literature, etc.

Of course, all this is purely academic! Today our world is what we have made it. For all practical purposes, it really doesn't matter how it all began (well maybe it does to physicists, astronomers, and biblical literalists). At least it does not matter, until some well meaning individual seeks to regain paradise-lost by trying to make modern society more like the purity, holiness, and innocence of Eden (as they understand it, I hasten to add). In the past, these attempts to regain Eden have ended in failure. We have a world that, for good or ill, will always be a mixture of the best and worst of which we humans are capable.

Although Genesis says that humankind gained the knowledge of good and evil, that is clearly incorrect. The whole of human history has aimed at knowing "right" from "wrong," and to judge from our ethical debates today, we still have a ways to go. So here we are, stuck in a world not of our beginning, but certainly of our own making, and the better part of wisdom is not to strive to bring in "God's kingdom." Such attempts in the past have succeeded in restricting human prospects, rather than enhancing them. We will never regain the innocence of Eden. Should we succeed in creating such a state, it will, more likely than not, turn out to be repressive, much like some early Christians thought the Garden of Eden was. Our American society may be secular, violent, and imperfect, but it is at least a society in which individuals may strive to reach their potential, and that pursuit for excellence (or holiness) seems far more interesting than waiting around for God to come calling in the cool of an Eden evening (Genesis 3:8).

⟨◈⟩

If the biblical texts are subject to such a wide range of interpretation, and they are, do they give us access to God or do they hinder us? Or put another way, does the Bible help us to know God's will? Many claim the Bible does give us access to God in a unique way, but we have had the Bible for an awfully long time and cannot seem to agree on what God really expects of us, even though in this country most of us use the Bible. Is there anyone *who knows what God expects of humankind?* If God communicates with human beings at all, it must be imperfectly—to judge by the radically different things we are told God expects of us. Exactly how do people who claim to know the divine mind encounter God? Does God speak audibly in the ear, inaudibly in the mind, or through "mental impressions"? People who claim to hear "voices," whether audible or mental, we usually lock away for treatment. But oddly, in western culture, we pay great deference to people who claim special access to divine counsel and who presume to tell us what God thinks about this or that.

In my religious tradition, the writers of the Bible are a special case. We Baptists (and I expect it is true of other denominations as well) might argue with the pastor, but we never argue with the Bible. Bible writers are immune to challenge, no matter what the text says. The Baptist view is that these writers received special messages from God in some way (audible voice? inaudible voice? mental impression?).

Some Baptists regard even the English words of modern translations as the very words God himself spoke, which, of course, could not be so, since the biblical languages are Hebrew, Aramaic, and Greek. If God actually "spoke" a human language (which is theoretically possible), his "literal" words would, therefore, be in Hebrew, Aramaic, and Greek. Of course, if God spoke in the ancient languages, he could also speak in modern languages, but we have no record of God ever doing that unless one assumes that the translators were "verbally" inspired. And given that there are so many different translations God seems to be sending different signals.

Questions arise also if divine communication is conceived as "mental impressions." Impressions are abstract and imprecise. God may be "sending" perfectly, but we humans have difficulty understanding our spouses even when we both speak the same language fluently. At the other extreme, some Baptists (probably not many) view the Bible merely as ancient texts, reflecting the culture, religion, and ethics of the past. Between these two attitudes (perfect words of God and flawed human impressions), lie multitudes of other attitudes.

The Bible has served our western culture well (for the most part), but it has also been used to authorize an array of unconscionable practices. During the Civil War, for example, southern religious leaders, using the Bible, justified slavery to their churches as God-ordained. The Bible's susceptibility to such unfortunate use makes one wonder how well tuned to the divine mind we and our own spiritual advisors actually are. For that matter, how well did even the Bible writers understand God? For example, surely Samuel, King Saul's spiritual advisor, misunderstood, when he told Saul God had ordered the utter destruction of the *Amalekites down to the last tiny infant (1 Samuel 15:1–3). God, of course, is like a 1200-pound Gorilla who can sit wherever he wants. But when God is described acting or speaking un-God-like, i.e., inconsistent with divine character or conscience, questions should arise about whoever describes him that way. Just maybe such people are not really fluent in God-speak after all. Be wary of people who know God's mind with absolute certainty, or even near certainty, because everything we know of God is influenced in some way by human finitude. Humility, not arrogant certainty, marks the honest prophet.

⊰◇⊱

Part of the problem of communication may be our translators and Bible experts. We are always subject to the mercy of the translator and since there is no such thing as translation without interpretation, we never really know how reliable they are. Here is an example that focuses itself with the question, *When did *Unicorns become wild oxen?*

Today the unicorn is legendary or mythical. But this was not always so. At one time the unicorn existed—or, at least, was thought to exist. As described in ancient scientific writings and depicted in painting and tapestry, the unicorn was a beautiful horse-like creature with a single long horn thought to have medicinal properties. Respected ancient scholars, such as *Aristotle (fourth century B.C.E: *Inquiry into Animals*) and *Pliny (first century C.E.: *Natural History*), mention them existing in their day. But today unicorns have gone the way of fairies, elves, and trolls. Belief in such creatures was abandoned with the eighteenth-century *Enlightenment. Oddly enough, however, the unicorn remained a fixture in the Bible until the nineteenth century. How could that possibly be? One may well ask.

Those ancient human beings who actually wrote the New Testament did not use the *Hebrew* Old Testament, but rather its *Greek translation* (the *Septuagint) as sacred Scripture. The Greek manuscripts of the Hebrew Bible are considerably earlier (fourth century) than the Hebrew (mostly tenth century). Unfortunately the Dead Sea Scrolls, although dating before the Common Era, have preserved for the most part only fragments of the

Hebrew Bible. In the Greek translation the following passages describe an animal having only one horn (*monokeros*) as a translation for the Hebrew word *re'em* (Numbers 23:22; Deuteronomy 33:17; Job 39:9–12; Psalms 22:21; 29:6; 77:69; 92:10; Isaiah 34:7). In the late fourth century, The Old Testament was translated into Latin (the *Vulgate) using both the Greek and Hebrew. In some of the passages listed above, the Vulgate translates the Hebrew *re'em* as "rhinoceros" and others as "unicorn" (both of these animals have only one horn). All Christians used the Vulgate until the sixteenth century, at which time *Martin Luther translated the Bible into German—the first time the Bible was ever translated into a modern European language. Luther used only the Hebrew, for the Old Testament. Nevertheless, he still translated *re'em* as unicorn. Later *William Tyndale, using only the Hebrew, likewise translated *re'em* as unicorn, and so did the King James Bible of 1611. In the nineteenth century, however, scholars decided that the Hebrew *re'em* did not really mean "unicorn," but rather "wild buffalo." Thus Christians from the fourth century well into the nineteenth found the (mythical?) unicorn in the Bible. The first English language edition to read "wild ox" for the Hebrew *re'em* was the American Standard Version of 1901! Today among Hebrew Bible scholars, "wild ox" has become the accepted English translation for *re'em*.

The *Greek Orthodox Church, however, still uses the ancient Greek version of the Jewish Bible as their Holy Scripture. Where it differs from the Hebrew (and it often does), they believe the differences are due to divine inspiration—meaning that the Greek updates the Hebrew. Unicorns, therefore, still exist in their Bible, as they existed for all Christians until the nineteenth and twentieth centuries. So the question boils down to this: Did scholars change *re'em* to "wild ox" because they knew unicorns were mythical or legendary and hence *should not/could not* have been in the Bible? Or did they change because of new information about the Hebrew word?

Once I asked a college class if they believed unicorns existed. They replied that unicorns had never existed—such is the influence of the *Enlightenment on western culture. But when I pointed out that unicorns were in the Bible until the nineteenth century (and still are in many Bibles), most students changed their minds—such is the influence of the Bible in modern life! What do you think? Were Christians misled by their Bibles for nineteen hundred years, or did unicorns really exist?

3. RELIGION, SELF, AND LIFE IN AMERICA

Religion, as I understand it, touches virtually on all areas of life. It extends from a casual passing conversation with a stranger, on the one hand, to formal acts of corporate worship, on the other. The essays in this section focus generally on subjects more in keeping with casual informality than with significant moments of moral crisis and ritual acts of formal worship.

In the streets people tend to think myopically, meaning that they are a bit nearsighted when it comes to their religious and social values, which they tend to associate with God and the Bible. In other words, in the popular view, American values originated with God; were it otherwise we would not hold to them. Our particular values were engrained in the genes of humanity at creation. Thus, all we need do is send missionaries to people who do not see things as we do, and these peoples of different views will be converted to our faith and values. The problem is, however, that our social and religious values appear to be the result of cultural engineering (not genetic engineering) and *are due simply to an accident of birth*, or so I concluded several years ago on the Greek island of Samos—it is rather difficult not to wax philosophical while smoking a good Dutch cigar, sipping a mellow Samian wine, and watching the moonrise over the *Aegean Sea. Our studio apartment over a "souper market" on the back side of the island was owned by a couple who had immigrated to Australia to raise their children. They came back to their village on Samos to re-open the market they inherited from Poppy's parents.

One of their two sons, Costas, came along to help with the eleven-hour days in the market. Costas spoke only a few words of Greek and that with a broad Australian twang. The situation of this family is typical of many Greek families in that small beach community. The tourists, on the other hand, were of several nationalities: German, Austrian, Scandinavian, Italian, and an occasional Brit—but only two Americans as far as I could tell, and certainly no other Baptists. And yet, except for their suntans and skimpy bathing suits, they looked little different from anyone you might meet at your local mall on a Friday night. They were different, however: different languages, customs, religions, hang-ups, taboos—and more.

I wondered whether people are inherently more alike than different, or inherently more different than alike? Because of Costas, I had to assume an inherent similarity among us all. In one sense we all entered the world as blank slates waiting to be inscribed with whatever language, religion, and culture our parents choose to endow us. At some point, of course, we start thinking for ourselves, but by that time we may be too far down life's road to change anything significant about our cultural codes. In that sense we are all alike—Ozarkians, Italians, American college professors, and Greek-Australian supermarket proprietors.

Religion, of course, is a BIG divider—perhaps the biggest. That fact has always struck me as odd. German and Swedish Lutherans, *Greek Orthodox, Roman Catholics, and Southern Baptists—we all worship the same God, use for the most part the same Bible and are products of the same religious history. But each of us tends to think of our God as somehow different—that "our God and religious customs are better than yours," one might say. Actually our Gods are the same. Values, the social codes by which we live, are things we can't compromise on, however. And so Peter and Poppy Francis, the supermarket proprietors, brought Costas back to Samos to find a nice Greek girl to marry—one reflecting those solid Greek family values they grew up with. But who is to say that Costas might not meet some nice Italian beauty in the Samian tourist world, and such a union would further complicate the cultural codes and religious values by which this particular family lives.

As I looked out at the world citizens who entered the supermarket beneath my balcony, I wondered about that too. Value systems and cultural codes are inherited as well as are first languages and supermarkets, and who is to say whose are better, or more meaningful? Except for an accident of birth to a Baptist mother who religiously enrolled me in a Mississippi Baptist Sunday school before I learned to walk, I might well have been a Greek Orthodox priest, rather than a Baptist minister.

Is it really true, as these somewhat unsettling reflections prompted by a Samian wine bottle suggest, that my most cherished values, my religion even, derive for the most part from the cultural circumstances of my birth? I don't know if I like that idea, since, like most readers, I tend to think that there is something absolute and enduring about my own religious traditions and cultural values. But if it is true, or even somewhat true, I probably ought to think a little more kindly of my brothers and sisters in the human family, any one of whom I might well have been, holding a different faith with as much certainty as I hold my own faith.

<hr />

Faith is very personal. What you believe in your heart of hearts cannot be mandated, no matter what public face you put on your faith. Faith is not a logical or mental thing, but likely lies closer to feeling than to rational logic. It is an attitude that people of all cultures and ethnic or national identities share. We all believe, or at least we all possess the innate capacity to believe in something. At bottom, faith is an attempt to breech the isolation and loneliness that always surrounds us in life. Even though we may be surrounded by friends and family, there is a part of us that is always inside and unknown to them. In life *we are like strangers in a foreign land*, as I was made aware on a business trip to Berlin back in the early 90s. Berlin is an awesome city! The guidebooks say that four cities the size of Paris can be accommodated in West Berlin alone. In such a city, one can well imagine the sense of anonymity that seizes anyone who wanders any distance from his or her own neighborhood.

If that is the case, undoubtedly even many Berliners have frequently felt like I felt every day. While riding the U-Bahn (German subway) each day to work in West Berlin from the eastern part of the city where I lived, I noted the almost visible walls of silence surrounding each commuter in my subway car. I sat quietly—for fear someone would say something to me in German that I would misunderstand, and be embarrassed by my lack of ability with the language. But it would be no different even if I spoke fluent German, since everyone rides in silence; no one speaks at 7.00 a.m. on the Berliner U-Bahn.

It is not just the hour; a sense of isolation seizes all riders—Germans and American—in the presence of strangers in very close quarters. We all retreated into silence, for communicating with strangers at such an early hour in tightly packed compartments requires considerable effort. It was just easier to remain silent for the short ride.

Perhaps we were silent because language—even one's own native language—is in many ways a barrier. All of us have experienced a frequent inability to express precisely what we think or feel, even to those closest to us. And if that is the case, we really are all alone in the world—at least to the extent we sense that no one ever completely knows our deepest thoughts and feelings. Perhaps that is why religious faith is such a big part of human life. Faith provides a nonverbal channel for expressing one's most intimate thoughts. In faith we sense that we can communicate in a completely satisfying way without words.

In my religious tradition, such a feeling is most apt to occur for me in worship through music or in silent meditation. At these moments I am free from the everyday requirements and restrictions of language. I do not need to struggle for words to express myself, but can communicate freely and perfectly at a nonverbal level. And when I make a mess of communicating with significant others (my wife, my children, my boss, my students), it is helpful to know that someone else understands.

But, of course, that does not facilitate communication on the job and in the streets, where we must frequently search for just the right words to express particular ideas or to put emotion into words. Under many circumstances, the spoken language fails us altogether or has an empty, hollow ring. At those times nonverbal language—a smile, a tear, a hug, a frown—says eloquently what mere words could never express. We humans use both "languages" to pierce the isolation that always surrounds us. Sometimes, however, silence is the better part of wisdom in spite of the isolation—like, for example, at seven in the morning on the Berliner U-Bahn.

Life may be "like a box of chocolates" as *Forrest Gump said, but it is definitely not like shopping down one side of a street and back up the other, as I tried to tell my wife in Athens, Greece one summer. "What do you want to do?" I asked her, as we stood at the top of Stadiou, a street of exclusive shops between Syntagma and Omonia squares in central Athens. "Shop down one side and back up the other," she replied. "But if you do that," I protested, "we won't be able to walk up Athinas," a street that runs through the Athens Central Market. "We don't have the time to do both."

Life is like that. Every choice closes off other possibilities that might have led into different and possibly unique life-changing experiences. What might you have become, for example, had you made different choices in your youth? What will you yet become—because there are always choices. There is not time enough to explore every opportunity and each choice leads into life experiences that help shape who you are and will become.

Many young people have not learned this lesson. They think they are immortal and see no limits to the possibilities and opportunities of life. If they miss one, they shrug and say, "There will be other opportunities." They think there will always be time enough and are not aware how each choice subtly shapes them, determining the course of their life, forever closing off possibilities and missed opportunities. But you really cannot blame them, since hindsight is always more clear for all of us, and there has to be a long enough course to a life for one to see its awkward twists and turns.

I had a good friend in high school who wanted to be a country-western singer. He had, and still had till the day of his death, the talent to make it happen. But at a critical juncture he went off to college majoring in chemistry, then to graduate school, a Ph.D., and a career as a research chemist at a major university. He was never really content, however, because deep down he wanted to do something else. Alas, a chemistry degree turned him into academia rather than show business and his music somehow got left behind in the turn.

That's the way life is. You begin, thinking you can have it all—i.e. shop both sides of streets with exclusive shops, but it is not really possible to do that. Every street you turn into leaves other streets unexplored. So choose your chocolates carefully. My wife was well content with shopping both sides of Stadiou Street. But me? I will always wonder what I missed that summer afternoon at the Athens Central Market on Athinas Street.

Philanthropy—sharing our "wealth" with those less fortunate than we, has an honored place in our society. Americans always respond generously to need, particularly in times of great human tragedy. The political administration in America from 2000–2008 recognized this generous trait and changed the rules on channeling government funds through non-profit organizations, particularly churches and other religious groups. Obvious problems with this policy exist, of course, but it at least recognizes the essential philanthropic role that religious organizations play in American society. Judaism and Christianity share a lengthy tradition of service to impoverished citizens in America, and others around the world. Many in these religious traditions give sacrificially from their own, often meager, resources to aid those worse off.

From what I read, however, the Christian tradition calls for much more. We Christians think of ourselves, in spite of our diversity in ecclesiastical organization and practice, as "followers of Jesus." The standard Jesus set for following him was very high indeed. On one occasion a wealthy man asked him, "What must I do to inherit eternal life?" Jesus responded with a rather long list of required religious obligations (Mark 10:18–19), all of which the man claimed he had always observed. Yet he lacked one thing: Jesus said: "Sell what you have and give to the poor and you will have treasure in heaven, and come follow me." Requiring this man to liquidate his holdings in order to follow suggests that Jesus himself is indigent, penniless, and must depend on God (viz. "give us this day our daily bread," Matthew 6:11) and the kindness of strangers for his daily sustenance. Apparently the wealthy man is being called to a life of itinerant poverty (for "the Son of Man had no place to lay his head," Luke 9:58). "How difficult it will be for the rich to enter the Kingdom of God" (Mark 10:25), Jesus said to his disciples. According to Luke, Jesus thought the Kingdom of God belonged to the poor (Luke 6:20), and even pronounced woes on the rich (6:24). Jesus commended a poor widow for her gift to the temple treasury. Her two copper coins, all she had it turns out, exceeded everything the "rich" contributed all together, for she gave "all the living she had" (21:1–4). Being rich and poor is relative, of course. You might not regard yourself as "rich" in a community having its wealthy philanthropists and university presidents, many drawing $250,000 plus perks or more per annum, but in impoverished third-world countries an American lower class income qualifies as "rich."

The point of this essay is to raise the following question: Since the gospel writers thought Jesus was quite clear on the call to penniless indigence, how do we twenty-first-century Christians with personal bank accounts, personal property, and investments, who belong to churches owning extensive facilities, property, bank accounts, and investments, incorporate such an impractical call into the current practice of our faith? I am much better with questions than answers, but what I have read on this issue leaves the following problem unresolved: the organization and practice of Christianity since the second century is quite different from the practice of Jesus and his itinerant band of associates in the first century. If what we practice is "Christianity," then Jesus and his band of mendicants were surely not Christians. Clearly the second-century church organizations we have adopted and modified are more practical than the itinerant model of Jesus. And this observation raises another: In what other ways have we "improved" on Jesus and what he taught?

⊸◈⊸

Would any God authorize violence in his name? Although the question may strike the reader as odd, apparently many people think so—and with justification I might add. The Hebrew Bible has many examples of violence, which God himself is said to have authorized. In 1995, Yitzak Rabin, the Prime Minister of Israel, was assassinated by a rabbinic student. If we are to believe the killer, God himself sanctioned the assassination of Rabin. Why did God tell him to do it, do you suppose—if indeed he did? Rabin was giving up Israeli land for peace. Many "Bible believing" Jews and Christians hold the deep-seated conviction that the land of *Canaan (i.e., *Palestine) was given to the ancient Israelites and their descendants as a perpetual inheritance (Genesis 12:1–3, 7; 17:8). How could Rabin so blatantly disobey God and the Bible by giving away what God had decreed belonged to the people of Israel forever?—so the rationale must have gone.

In recent years we have witnessed an escalation of public violence, including a surprising public rhetoric of violence, in the name of religion. Who will ever forget the footage on the evening news of the *Ayatollah

Khomeini leading thousands of Iranian *Muslims in chants of "Death to the Great Satan" (that is, America)? In our own country certain individuals, active in the anti-abortionist movement, translated the rhetoric of violence into action. They murdered physicians who performed abortions—and the killers claimed divine sanction for their deeds. Even AIDS was declared by some conservative religious leaders in America, with the tacit approval of their flocks, as God's judgment on homosexuals. Unfortunately such raw violence is not unique. The course of history is littered with terrorism and extremism, whose "true believers" claimed to hear the voice of God as justification for their aberrant and violent behavior. Fortunately most citizens are level headed enough not to take such radical claims seriously; they condemn such acts and the violent rhetoric for what it is, and simply do not believe that God is a terrorist. The main streams of Christianity, Judaism, and Islam at their noblest abhor and condemn both terrorist language and violence committed in God's name.

Unfortunately, however, the God of these major western religions has something of a checkered past, to judge from certain narratives in the Bible and the *Qur'an. These violent stories may in part explain why some people are prone to credit God with the strange voices they hear. For some people the Bible, thought to be God's Holy Word, justifies violence. For example, God "allowed" Satan to ravage Job's life, possessions, and even kill his children as a test of Job's faith (Job 1); God himself killed Korah, Dathan, and Abiram and their families because these three men disagreed with and opposed Moses and Aaron (Numbers 16). Samuel, the prophet of the Lord, told Saul that God commanded him to "utterly destroy" all of the *Amalekites, sparing nothing and no one (1 Samuel 15). God is portrayed as destroying the entire cities of Sodom and Gomorrah because of their "sins and wickedness" (Genesis 18–19). Elijah, the prophet, killed 450 prophets of Baal because their religion was not a "true faith" (1 Kings 18). There are other similar stories; these do not exhaust the number of terrorist-like acts in the Bible credited to the God of Judeo-Christian faith. Of course, most people would not assume that such stories authorize murders and assassinations, but there are those in society who do use them to justify their intolerance and violence.

There is a certain naïveté on the part of many of our citizens about God, the Bible, and religion that makes them vulnerable to religious quacks, confidence men (and women), the delusional, the militant "true believer," and the good-hearted but misguided soul who has a need to control the lives of others. Because religion deals with "unseen realities," there are many opportunities for "flim flam" and "sleight of hand." How is a person to know the genuine thing from the counterfeit? How is one to know whether the broker dealing in religious faith (i.e., the pastor, priest, rabbi, imam, preacher, Bible teacher) is legitimate? Indeed, what legitimizes a religious leader? Is it "ordination" by an organized church, synagogue, or mosque? Is it the Bible? These guides will not always work, since the abuse of the public in America is frequently perpetrated specifically by the church's use of the Bible. The surest way to gain a following among the naive and religiously illiterate is by quoting the Bible, or being sanctioned by a church, and claiming to know what God wants.

The public can protect itself from those who use religion for their own ends only by becoming literate in matters religious and developing a healthy skepticism. Not all who quote the Bible or wear the collar can be trusted, particularly when they claim to know God's will for others. Some who take upon themselves the mantle of religious leadership are more responsible and better equipped for the task than others. Individuals must learn to evaluate their prophets and to assume personal responsibility for deciding their own religious obligations. They must wrestle with the question of God's will for their lives in both its broad outlines and in its minutiae, rather than surrendering this responsibility to the religious professional or the charismatic true believer. Most importantly, people must learn to weigh the value of religious ideas to which they are exposed through media evangelism and even in their own family religious institutions. Not all religious ideas have the same value.

Basically citizens must gain control of their own religious lives and not allow themselves through guilt and ignorance to be caught up in the agendas of others, no matter how worthy the project may seem. Always be suspicious of anyone who knows with absolute clarity what God wants. Through their vision, enthusiasm, and self-confidence such people can eventually gain control of the lives of others. Even those who invoke God's name for basically good causes have an interest in involving others in their projects.

Knowing God's will for the lives of others is something that only an extremist will claim with certain clarity. And it was an extremist that robbed Israel of the leadership of Yitzhak Rabin: freedom fighter, soldier, patriot, statesman, and man of peace. Religious extremism in any form for whatever reason is no virtue, because it always deprives people of the prerogatives of their own lives. The murder of Yitzhak Rabin is a graphic example.

⊰◈⊱

We all need places of retreat in the mind—a place for each of us that holds the promise of a respite from the pressures of life, if even for a single moment. A seventeenth-century philosopher, *Rene Descartes, asserted: "I think; therefore I am." In his view the certainty of human existence lies in consciousness. Our very existence as human beings is centered in the mind. The realities outside us are given their shape, color, feel, and meaning within our minds, for things are as we perceive them to be, and our perceptions are never exactly the same as those of others.

When we choose, we can completely shut ourselves off from outside impressions and turn inward. For instance, we can escape into our minds when polite conversation turns boring and think above the process as observer rather than participant. In our minds we can relive the past or escape into invented fantasies. Such escapes and mental time travel are bittersweet, however; for at some point healthy minds must return to commonly perceived reality and boring conversation.

Occasionally we all need to shut out the perceptive world, particularly when stressors at home, on the job, or in other social contexts become too much to face at any given moment. Stress eventually catches up with all of us to some degree, and for those moments we need special places in the mind. My *Shangri-La is a mental retreat to some out of the way Greek island at moonrise over *Homer's "wine-dark sea." The brief reverie helps me regain perspective and refresh the spirit. On the other hand, there are places in the mind we had rather not go—into the dark secrets of our lives, the ugly moments, and painful experiences. Such black holes lurk about in every mind—though we keep them as far out of consciousness as possible.

In all religions exists an ideal place where believers expect to find ultimate deliverance from the rigors of living in a less than ideal world. For Christians it is heaven, *Muslims call it *Paradise, for Buddhists it is *Nirvana, for ancient Greeks and Romans it was the *Elysian Fields. Such blessed states unquestionably "exist," in the minds of true believers—though by their very nature, they do not exist spatially and geographically, like the planet Mars exists, for example. Nevertheless, the human spirit needs such ultimate retreats where the scales of justice are finally balanced and eternal rest from the toil and trouble of an imperfect world is realized.

One can have too much "heaven" on the mind, however, particularly if it leads to escapism or religious autism. With the world forgotten: an Islamic "martyr," wired for detonation, is already mentally dwelling in Paradise; enraptured Christians, arms uplifted, have retreated into heavenly bliss; cloistered monks shut the world out and are totally absorbed in meditation, beads, and hypnotic chants—each in retreat from our failed *Eden, a blue and white bramble patch in a backwater of the *Milky Way, too much heaven on their minds; each trying to escape the common lot of humanity: pain, thorns, thistles, and sweat (Genesis 3:16–19). Nevertheless, even bramble patches grow roses, and in the final analysis a pruned bramble patch with the odd rose will always trump Eden in the mind.

❧◈❧

Several years before I retired, I was so caught up in an active academic career, involved in campus life, community activities, and professional activities that I felt like my very soul was at risk. Somewhere between Los Angeles, California (where I completed a Ph.D. in 1977) and Springfield, Missouri (where I retired from Missouri State University in 2005), *my soul seemed to have gone missing*, or was so shriveled I had trouble finding it. Souls need special feeding and watering to flourish. I suspect that I am not the only person to come to this realization.

You might not think it possible for a man to lose his soul, but Jesus seemed to think so. "What is the profit," he said, "in gaining the world and losing your soul" (Mark 8:36). Charles Dickens also thought so, and in his novel, *A Christmas Carol*, portrayed Ebenezer Scrooge as a soulless man, who actually rediscovers his soul at the end of the story. "Soul" is the essence of being truly human—a quality always pushing us, come hell or high water, toward moral excellence. A man or a woman with no soul has lost the qualitative edge of being human, of keeping life in balance and everything in proper perspective—in other words, "losing yourself to gain the world" (Luke 9:25) distorts perspective and throws life into serious imbalance. Clearly Scrooge was disoriented. He had fed his soul so much material "stuff" that he totally lost touch with his humanity. In my case, somewhat like *Bob Cratchit, I sat in a tiny windowless office (until late in my career) cluttered with neglected professional projects (real soul food, by the way), and fed my soul unimaginative papers by incurious students, and interminable pieces of, apparently necessary, organizational paper, but in the grand scheme of things virtually irrelevant. Souls can't survive on such an unbalanced diet.

Can governments lose their souls? Certainly! Government at every level involves people who set the government's tone and carry out its policies. *National Socialism in Hitler's Germany, at best, was government without conscience, but its systematic massacre of Jews and other eastern Europeans clearly qualifies it as soulless. The same is true of *Saddam Hussein's Iraqi government, for attempting to annihilate its own citizens, the Kurds. In our own country, the suppressive disfranchisement (and worse!) of black citizens in the Deep South for over one hundred years can only be explained by the shriveled souls of white citizens. And what should we say about attempts in various states to eliminate budgetary support for our most vulnerable citizens—the mentally ill, disabled, children, and the elderly? At best, it is not an action to be confused with moral excellence.

Can a church lose its soul? You wouldn't think so, but in my religious tradition it has been happening for some time now. For the sake of what some regard as "right theology," Southern Baptist intolerants dismantled a fellowship of more or less independent cooperating churches, centralized their authority, and have been since 1985 purging the denomination of diversity. Shortening the borders of the tent and shallow thinking make for better control, but will not encourage the development of healthy souls.

Without a healthy soul, we never find our way to the moral high road, or, as Paul put it, to the more excellent way (1 Corinthians 12:31—13:13). Without soul we are condemned "to sit among mattresses of the dead" (*Wallace Stevens, "The Man on the Dump")." Allowing a soul to shrivel away is bad enough. Being unaware of it altogether is a crisis of epic proportions.

Why do I exist? Why am I here? These are not exactly the same questions, but they are certainly related. The first addresses reality (why does anything exist at all—including me). The other is an intensely personal question (for what reason have I come to this particular point in life). Looking out over the *Libyan Sea into the abyss of a pitch-black *Cretan night from my balcony in the tiny, almost non-existent, Greek village of Kalamaki, I pondered the fates that had conspired to bring me to this particular spot on this particular night.

In the grand scheme of things is there a particular purpose for every human being? In 1859, *John Brown, convinced he was an instrument in the hands of God to free the slaves, attacked the Federal Armory and Arsenal at Harpers Ferry, Virginia. The forty-third President of the United States, George W. Bush, has been described in similar "chosenness" language. As a religious man, he is convinced that the mission of engaging and defeating terrorism is his "divinely inspired" manifest destiny.[1] These ideas of divine mission are not unlike a great one-liner in the Bible story of Esther. Queen Esther (a Jew) was asked by her uncle Mordecai to inform the Persian King (Esther's husband) about a plot to annihilate all Judeans in the *Persian Empire. Esther at first demurred on the grounds that going to the king without first being summoned could result in her death. Mordecai suggested she perhaps held the position of queen by divine design: "Who knows," he said "perhaps you have come to royal dignity for just such a time as this" (Esther 4:14). Was Mordecai correct? Is there an overarching divine purpose for each of us? Do we all have a right place at a right time? Mordecai thought it possible, but was not sure. And who really knows? Mordecai only recognized that Esther had an opportunity to save her people from annihilation.

Pastors and seminary professors have assured me many times that the chief end of human beings is to serve and praise God. I take that to be a generic answer to the first question, because it is not very "me-specific." I suspect they were trying to tell me that my responsibility as a Christian lay in serving God in the context of the community of faith. (Somehow these questions are always seen in practical terms by the priestly functionaries of the church!) So, they reassure me, I serve God through the agencies of MY church and worship him in ITS formal rituals and services. But *Abraham was not Christian, neither was *Muhammad, nor *Buddha.

Not even Jesus was Christian (he was actually Jewish). Then how could it be that what I was told is in the final analysis the chief end of all humanity, if that obligation could not possibly fit every human being?

But my question was not why am I (as a human being) here; it was why am I—me myself—here? My question was very personal and me-specific. One pastor once suggested that because of my background and training (Baptist college and Seminary) I should be teaching in a Baptist College rather than a state university, because I could best serve God in that capacity. I have always wondered if that pastor was implying that teaching in a Baptist educational institution was somehow a higher calling than serving the citizens of the state by teaching in a state university. Apparently teaching in one context was Christian service and in the other, for some odd reason, was merely public service.

Some people seem to know from an early age exactly what they will do with their lives—although their planned destinies do not always materialize. Many of us, if we are lucky, discover our comfort zones midway through the course of our lives and we just accept what the fates have sent us. Some never do, but for various reasons end up in situations they never anticipated, trapped in a web of circumstances seemingly beyond their control.

We can never know the reason for our personal existence (or even if there is a reason) for certain, though we may think we do. If the reason for my existence can be known at all, it is only in retrospect. Others (like Mordecai) are more than willing to tell us why we are here. Historians do this all the time in their histories of the rich and famous. In truth, however, making sense of our lives will likely be done for us by friends, and family—or the priests/ministers/rabbis/imams who recite eulogies at funerals. Few of us, like Mordecai, John Brown, and George Bush, are able to know with absolute clarity the defining moment of our lives—if there is a single defining moment. Truth be told, there are likely many such moments in every life. Even if we recognized them all, we would likely not be willing to pay full price for making them so. Queen Esther and John Brown were willing—and apparently so was George W. We can only pray he listened to the right voices.

Perhaps there is no completely satisfactory answer to the question "why am I here?" Maybe there is not a single purpose predestined for individuals in particular. Your life is what you make of it. And when you reach the twilight of your years and look back then you might begin to make some sense out of your life—but it is only in retrospect. There is no overarching scheme into which you as an individual must fit. If that is correct (and I freely admit it may not be), then we must make the most of life each day we live. There is really no definitive answer to the question "why am I here." You are here. The rest is up to you.

❦

In the last few years all religious denominations in America have been struggling with the same philosophical differences that have divided the country into red and blue states. Two of the most prominent church bodies to be so separated are the Episcopalian Church, over the appointment of a gay bishop, and the Southern Baptist Convention over the issue of diversity in the churches of the convention.

In 1998 the Southern Baptist Convention amended the 1963 Southern Baptist Faith and Mission Statement to read in part: "A wife is to submit graciously to the servant leadership of her husband even as the church willingly submits to the headship of Christ." This statement ("wives submit yourself to your husbands," cf. Ephesians 5:22–24) politicizes the New Testament rather than clarifying its diverse views on the relationship of men and women, husbands and wives. Forces afoot in the Southern Baptist Convention over the last twenty-five years have aimed at eradicating diversity in the independent churches supporting the activities of the national convention, in part by turning a general statement of faith endorsed by a majority of delegates to the convention into a creedal confession binding on all Southern Baptists. Baptists, in general, have traditionally rejected creeds and opted instead for what they call "the priesthood of the believer," meaning that individual Baptists have the right to resolve issues of faith for themselves. Thus this amendment is a move in the direction of creed.

The relationship of husbands and wives, men and women, in the New Testament is more complex than the amendment suggests. The Southern Baptist Convention slogan, "wives submit yourselves to your husbands," in Ephesians 5:22 is preceded by the more inclusive statement that husbands and wives should be submissive to one another (Ephesians 5:21), a view consistent with the Apostle Paul's slightly more democratic views regarding the relationship between men and women. Paul seems to have preferred that men and women be interdependent. For example, he argues from Genesis 2:22 that the biblical order of creation (woman originating from man) placed her under the authority of her husband (1 Corinthians 11:9). But Paul's real view seems to be that men and women ideally are interdependent, for the order of creation is now reversed, and in birth man originates from woman (1 Corinthians 11:11–12).

Paul's clearest statement is that the social distinctions prevalent in *Hellenistic society in the first century are eradicated in the church, and men and women are equal before God (Galatians 3:28). He fails, however, to specify in a later similar statement (1 Corinthians 12:13) that gender distinctions are eliminated. And unfortunately, the later followers of Paul (compare Colossians 3:11) were more influenced by this latter view, which was more representative of Hellenistic society in general.

Paul regarded women as colleagues (not underlings) in his ministry. See the high regard in which he held his women colleagues in Romans 16:1–16, where he commends the work of several women, among them the female deacon Phoebe; and his "fellow worker," Prisca, who had risked her life for him; and the eminent woman apostle, Junia (Romans 16:7). Compare this attitude with that of the author of First Timothy, who had such a low view of women that he argued "a woman will be saved through bearing children, if she continues in faith, love, and holiness with modesty" (1 Timothy 2:13–15). Paul's later followers, writing books in his name, appropriated the general ethical values of Hellenistic society.

The annual meeting of Southern Baptists has for some time been a forum for realizing political agendas. By bringing the Baptist Faith and Message Statement more in line with the views of those intolerant of diversity in the churches, they have intended to influence the ideological makeup of local churches. Hopefully when the footlights dim and the spotlights are turned off, Baptist pastors will be more balanced and responsible in their local ministries, and churches will continue to encourage the diversity of views that have been hallmarks of Baptist life in the past. A majority vote at the annual meeting does not automatically translate into a majority of all Southern Baptists.

⊰◇⊱

Can a critical thinker also be a person of traditional religious faith? True, many are, or at least appear to be—but who knows what goes on in another's mind. As a purely theoretical question, the answer must be: "maybe." Two variables skew the response: the thinker's curiosity and the reasonableness of the article of faith. Faith may not demand that *critical* thinkers affirm something they know to be patently false. Critical thinkers by their very nature are curious, leading them to evaluate and critique the evidence before making a decision—or a faith commitment. Curiosity is the mother's milk of critical thinking—without it there will be no critical thought.

Conservative religion in western culture, however, offers its propositional truths as paradigmatically *absolute*—the product of divine revelation, to be questioned only at the risk of one's immortal soul. Nevertheless, critical thinkers are typically not so generous as to affirm without critiquing. Regardless of the stakes, an individual who suppresses curiosity and accepts a religious proposition without serious challenge is not thinking critically.

The real difficulty with religious truths, however, is that the absolute religious truth of one group frequently refutes the absolute religious truth of another. Here is an example of one divine truth canceling another. Roman Catholics regard the wine and bread of the Mass as the *actual* body and blood of Christ. Lutherans reject this view but affirm that in some way Christ is *truly present* in the bread and wine of the Eucharist. Baptists and others, on the other hand, regard the bread and grape juice (not wine!) of the Lord's Supper as merely symbolical, only *representing* the body and blood of Christ. As long as such ideas as these are considered simply different "beliefs" among religious groups, it is merely an oddity prompting the response: odd, how can people in the same religion using the same holy books believe such remarkably different things? But when it is remembered that these three groups hold that their respective views are absolutely binding on believers as the product of divine wisdom, it should strike a critical thinker as a curiosity worthy of further investigation—particularly into the assumptions made by each group. Of course, they cannot all be the result of divine revelation! But the solution is not as easy as determining which is right and eliminating the other two.

The problem really goes to the nature of "religious truth." Religious truth is not objective like mathematics—like $2 + 2 = 4$, for example. Rather religious truth is subjective in every case. Like beauty, religious truth lies in the eye, or in this case mind, of the beholder. The absolute character of the religious proposition exists only in the mind of the believer who holds it, although true believers are scarcely apt to agree. Such regimentation and uncritical perspective is apt to strike the critical thinker as curious—if not a bit suspicious.

✦

Watching the rising of a full moon on a clear crisp winter evening can create a magical moment for those who pause to watch it pass across the sky. The light of a full moon turns night into day, farm boys into poets, and wallflowers into roses. Its magic works, even though we know the moon does not rise. Rather, the earth's rotation around the sun creates an illusion of moonrise. And the moon does not shine. Rather, moonshine is reflected sunlight that has traveled 150 million kilometers (about 90 million miles) at a speed of 186,000 miles per second to reach our tiny blue and white planet. Even at that rate of speed, the distance is so great that sunlight still takes eight minutes to reach the earth. But in terms of the uncharted reaches of space the distance to the sun is of little significance.

Our universe is still expanding at an incredible rate of speed, and we inhabitants of a small planet in an out-of-the-way galaxy are being carried with it to some unknown rendezvous. We do not know the precise age of earth, but it existed millennia before the Gods of earth heard their first prayers. From this cosmic perspective, the fixed beliefs and values separating us tend to lose some of their significance. Reflecting on our differences in the moonlight just might encourage more of us to seek common ground on those divisive issues we persist in fighting about: racial, religious, cultural, ethical, and political. We are all members of the human family regardless of skin color, religious commitment, and national origin. Our differences, that seem so un-resolvable in the heat of debate, are not nearly as great as the earth's distance from the sun. And in the magic of moonlight on a winter's evening even the most controversial of these differences seems like the distance from Los Angeles to New York—when viewed in the light of earth's position in the universe. From a cosmic perspective we cantankerous humans do not appear to be that far apart. We would do well to remind ourselves that today's burning social issues become tomorrow's benign history lessons. From a historical perspective, they tend to move us to quiet reflection and exam preparation rather than to the soapbox and civil unrest. History is littered with the skeletons of out-of-date causes to die for, but now they are little more than curious ideas of our historical past.

If we cannot learn to love and respect each other in spite of the diverse views we hold, we could at least learn to tolerate our diversity amicably. We live on such a small planet awash in an unfathomable sea of space (a thousand earths could fit inside Jupiter!). There are no other planets, at least not in our local neighborhood that can support our kind of life, and so far as we now know, we are alone in the universe. But that could easily change. In the light of earth's isolation and provincialism, therefore, we need one another—in spite of our differences and diverse allegiances. In the larger scheme of things a little patience and more humility may not close the ideological gaps that separate us, but they could at least help to reduce tensions and bring us closer together.

On the next clear evening, step out in the backyard and track the moon for a bit. A little "moonshine" just might improve your communal temperament.

4. DOES ABSOLUTE TRUTH EXIST?

Is there a true religion? In many ways this is a very interesting question, because every person of faith assumes their religion is true; otherwise they would not affirm it. But religions come and go. For example, *Hellas, the land of the ancient Greeks, once belonged to *Zeus. Near the dawn of human memory, a land belonged to the God who was worshiped there (remember how Jonah tried to flee from the Israelite God, *Yahweh, by running to another land?). When Zeus was born in a cave on Mount Ida on the Greek island of *Crete, the land belonged to the *Great Mother Goddess (her personal name is unknown, as are her cult and rituals). She was the dominant deity in the Cretan *Minoan culture (roughly 3500 to 1100 B.C.E.), but eventually Zeus and his *Olympians replaced her in the hearts of the people. For over 1000 years, Zeus (Jupiter as the Romans called him) was Lord throughout the Mediterranean basin in the Greek and Roman periods (roughly 800 B.C. to 325 C.E.). Zeus and Yahweh required blood sacrifices from their worshipers, a practice that continued in Judean state religion until the destruction of the Jerusalem temple in 70 C.E. Even the great Christian missionary, Paul, went to the Jerusalem temple and publicly declared his intent to offer the required sacrifices to Yahweh well after his conversion to Christianity (Acts 21:18–29; cf. Numbers 6:9–12).

Zeus' power was not seriously challenged until the fourth century C.E., when the Roman emperor, *Constantine, endorsed the worship of the Christ, who had been born a Jewish lad under the name Jesus some 300 years earlier in the Judean village of Bethlehem. From that time, Zeus's power and prestige diminished as that of the Christ grew. Eventually the *Roman Empire became a Christian state, governed by church authority. And it survived as the Holy Roman Empire until the *Middle Ages. And today, as then, in Greece there is still no separation of church and state. The Christ who reigns in Greece is the Lord of Eastern *Orthodox Christianity, however. How he is conceived and worshiped in the Christian east (in Orthodoxy) is rather different from how he is conceived and worshiped in western Christianity (Roman Catholic and Protestant traditions). Our western brand of Christianity emerged from Europe following the *Protestant Reformation and the *Counter-Reformation of the sixteenth century, and has been heavily influenced by western philosophical thought. Orthodoxy in the east, on the other hand, is far more introspective and mystical, and much less influenced by western philosophy.

This rise and fall of Gods and religions in Greece suggests that the religion of any people is actually shaped by the social conditions under which they live. In other words, the Gods we worship and what we regard as true religion depends largely on when and where we were born. Or put another way, true religion is whatever my own personal confession happens to be. For example, if I am a committed Baptist, other Baptists would likely regard me a heretic should I find Roman Catholicism a truer approach to Christian faith. For good or ill, religions compete with one another, and particularly in a missionary religion like Christianity, even its various denominations compete with one another for recognition as the true version of Christianity. There are even splits within denominations over which faction represents the true version of the faith, as the current struggle in the Southern Baptist Convention clearly attests.

Sadly, even though all Christian groups have much in common, they seem to focus only on their differences. For example, Baptists, in general, think that Catholics and the Orthodox (when they think of them) are wrong both in theology and the practice of their faith. The Orthodox and the Roman Catholics, of course, think they do it right. On the other hand, to a Roman Catholic, Baptists are, at best, woefully misguided, and thus terribly mistaken in faith and practice. But despite their disagreements, both Baptists and Roman Catholics would likely agree that the Orthodox Church ("Orthodox" means "right belief," by the way) has completely missed the mark, as far as being a true version of Christianity is concerned. And, of course, the Orthodox have the same opinion about Baptists and Roman Catholics. All of this raises the question: are there no absolutes in religion? Of course there are! Just ask the Baptists, the Roman Catholics, and the Orthodox!

<hr />

It is somewhat ironic to note that Christianity began in the first century literally as a religion of the "new age"—early Christian preaching claimed that Jesus began a "new age" for the world. It is also ironic to note that for the first two hundred fifty years of its existence Christianity was a pro-scribed religion and, hence, had to exist underground. When the Roman emperor *Constantine converted to Christianity, he stopped the official persecution of Christians in the west (313 C.E). Christianity eventually became the sanctioned religion of the empire and surprisingly turned to treating other religions as it had formerly been treated.

In the final analysis, proscription and censorship did not work against early Christianity in its underground period and it will not work today. Whoever seeks official community sanction for their particular religious views should realize that the community cannot control what people believe. The reason is that an idea is a force whose power lies in its appeal to the human imagination. What people believe helps them make sense of their lives and the world about them; such ideas cannot be stopped. Any religion that feels it must censor the religious ideas of others could well be on the brink of intellectual bankruptcy. The battle for hearts and minds cannot, in the final analysis, be won by guns, political legislation, censorship, proscription, or community sanctions. That battle can be won only by better, and more convincing, ideas.

The public schools of this nation should not endorse one religious faith over another. Rather the schools should be a "free market" for ideas. In our schools, students ought to be provided with the opportunity to find out about the world including information about all religions—as those religions understand themselves. Ideally, public schools do not deal in absolute truths; rather they deal in truths whose content changes as new information emerges. Dry desert sands and the dusty stacks of old libraries continue to turn up information about our past affecting how historians understand the religious roots of western civilization.

A religion that tries to sweep the field of its competitors by censoring competing ideas, or by suppressing new information about religious origins eventually will marginalize itself as a viable religious option in the modern world. Such a strategy can work, if only temporarily, in a totalitarian state. It will not work in a democracy. Our children do not need protection from nontraditional religious ideas. They need to be trained to think critically so that they can evaluate the merits of all religious ideas for themselves, including those held by their parents and the religious professionals. In the final analysis, the only way to protect students from bad ideas and religious charlatanism of any stripe is to teach them to make judgments in the light of evidence—that is, to think critically. Religious ideas that fail to inspire the human imagination are not going to be shored up by censorship. Christians ought to know that, since it was the appeal of the Christian gospel to the human imagination that really captured the *Roman Empire.

⊷◈⊶

Many religious denominations of a more conservative bent have a less than admirable record on academic freedom in their educational institutions. "Academic freedom" is a policy extending to teachers the liberty to think, teach, and publish without being censored. The only limit to academic freedom is this: professors cannot advocate illegal activity, though they may think about it, and explore the "what if" in their classrooms and publications.

In conservative denominational colleges and universities a limited academic freedom does exist, but not without proscriptions. For example, certain issues have always been exempted, that is, the "sacred cows" of conservative religious faith, such as the nature of the Bible, homosexuality, and human origins. In seminaries and liberal arts colleges controlled (politically and financially) by the denomination, teaching and writing about such issues have defined limits, which a professor may cross only at the risk of job and career.

Up to a point, one must admit that some limits seem reasonable, particularly with regard to denominational seminaries. Seminaries are funded by the denomination to train pastors and other church workers. Every denomination has a right to expect that their seminary graduates will be suitable to serve the denomination in positions of leadership. Nevertheless, they claim the right to educate along ideological lines at the loss of academic freedom, which becomes merely an illusion in schools that limit free inquiry. Ideological education, known by its less popular but more accurate name, is "indoctrination." Today the situation has grown worse. In the Southern Baptist Convention (SBC), for example, before 1985, a modicum of diversity was tolerated. Since 1985, the ideological leaders of the SBC have deliberately purged the denomination of diversity by virtually any means possible.

In Kansas City, Missouri, in 1961, Midwestern Baptist Seminary Professor Ralph H. Elliott published a small book with the SBC publisher (Broadman) titled *The Message of Genesis*. The book said nothing not being said in mainstream seminaries and colleges around the world; in some contexts this particular book would likely have even been labeled "conservative." After vigorous objections to the book arose in the SBC, Broadman Press recalled the book from distribution, and Professor Elliott lost his job. He crossed the "nature of the Bible" line in the sand. Later another press republished the book; they said, "in the name of religious and academic freedom"—a sad commentary on Baptist education in the SBC and Missouri Baptist Convention.

In 2003 leaders of the Missouri Baptist Convention (MBC) demanded that *William Jewell College (a private liberal arts college with historical ties to the SBC) clarify its teaching position on the biblical account of creation, take a strong stand against homosexuality, and accept trustees appointed by the MBC—a blatant political attempt to co-opt the educational program of the college. The Board of Trustees of William Jewell College declined, and the MBC cut off financial support to the college, which amounted to 3.3 percent of the school's budget. Basically, the Convention tried to censor free inquiry with its "thirty pieces of silver." To its credit, the school's board held that academic freedom was not for sale. The leaders of the MBC failed to appreciate the value of academic freedom—something censors always fail to do.

We get no choice about natural parents or our first language, culture, or religion. Yet these very things determine what we are taught, what we eventually come to believe, and the values we learn to cherish—in short, they determine who we become. In the final analysis, changing religion, for adults, is about as difficult as changing our genetic codes. It does happen, but not easily or often.

This observation raises the theoretical question: why try to convert people from one religion to another, anyway? I do not mean changing Christian denominations, even though that is difficult enough in some ways. I mean completely different religions—like a Presbyterian becoming *Muslim, or *Hindu (or vice versa).

The claim that "my religion is the true religion" cuts both ways. The claim to possess ultimate truth about God is made by all religions. All people think their religion is true. Why would anyone confess a religious faith they think is false? Thus, one religion's claim to have ultimate religious truth will always be trumped by other religions making exactly the same claim.

The qualitative difference of one religion (or Christian denomination) over another can reasonably be assessed only in terms of what each does to enhance and improve the lives of its followers. A religion that manipulates people for whatever reason, or limits freedom to experience God according to individual conscience, is suppressive. Actually, all religions (including my own) are guilty to some extent of using people for their own self-aggrandizement.

Much of the behavior touted by religious leaders as indicators of "genuine spirituality" constitutes, in the final analysis, limitation of religious liberty that the rank and file of the faith either ignore or juggle with difficulty—for example, the prohibition against a woman braiding her hair, wearing gold and pearls, and costly attire (1 Timothy 2:9), and Paul's odd argument that women be veiled in Christian worship (1 Corinthians 11:4–10). Such irrelevant behaviors are designed to reinforce an "in-group" mentality, and ultimately the economic viability and influence of the religion (or denomination).

Perhaps, it can be shown that one religion, over time, has a better track record in the treatment of its followers than others. But is it really fair to judge any religion on the basis of its extremists—to judge Christianity on the actions of a *Jim Jones and the sad events at *Jonestown, for example? All religions (and denominations, for that matter) have skeletons in their theological closets.

Probably the only intellectually defensible reason for "evangelizing" Muslims to Christian faith (or vice versa), or Methodists to Baptist faith (or vice versa), is because of a sincere desire to share a deeply felt religious experience. The desire "to share" is commendable. But the invitation to join "my religion," whatever it is, cannot convincingly be based on the claim of having ultimate truth, for all religions make that claim, and have the religious texts to prove it. True believers of all religious stripes are scarcely apt to agree, however.

⌘

What does it mean to "tolerate" another's views? Many from the Christian "right" think an encouragement to tolerate other views is a leftist attack upon their own beliefs. In this attitude one senses the frustration felt by deeply religious people who find their moral values marginalized by the "establishment." In their view they are required to "tolerate," which to them means "to accept, affirm, and support" behaviors they find morally reprehensible. The word "tolerate" resonates differently, however, for the more moderate center. Toleration has a more neutral significance; it means to adopt a "live and let live," attitude toward the ideas and behavior of others, if their behavior falls within the bounds of the law.

Tolerance is an essential aspect of American democracy. Our country is religiously and culturally diverse, and we continue to be a nation of immigrants. Allowing others with different value systems to live their lives in peace, so long as they live within the law, is absolutely essential to the survival of America as a pluralistic society. Under our present constitution we are all permitted to live lifestyles that some may find objectionable. Even if some consider these behaviors to be against "God's law" (as some may understand it), they are still permitted by the constitution so long as they fall within the limits of American legal codes.

America is not a Christian nation, or even a Judeo-Christian nation, based on biblical law, however much many may wish it to be. It has a system of secular law based on a constitution drafted to allow as much diversity and personal freedom as possible, particularly in the area of faith and morals. The constitution promotes human, not Christian, values and protects personal liberties. Majority rule creates a system generally permissive of diverse values. Even though some of us do not always agree with the majority, we at least see the wisdom of the system and therefore are able to tolerate the diversity in moral values. Problems surface when the more rigorous values of various minority groups collide with the broad-based lowest common denominator values of the rest of the community.

What strikes me as odd about the debate over tolerance in the Missouri Ozarks is that it is the Christian "right" objecting to tolerance as a community value, for Jesus demanded a much higher standard than tolerance. "Love your enemies" (Matthew 5:44), he said. What does it mean to love? Paul said "Love does not insist on its own way . . . love bears all things . . . endures all things" (1 Corinthians 13:4–7). I wonder what the Christian "right" would think of that concept as a community value?

Many people believe only one God exists (monotheism), and consider multiple Gods (*polytheism) impossible. Widespread belief in one God, however, is rare, and late, in history. The earliest recorded deviation from polytheism occurred in fourteenth-century B.C.E. Egypt. The God-King *Akhenaten worshipped *Aten, (represented by a sun-disc) while the Egyptians, formally at least, worshipped Akhenaten and Aten. Even the ancient Israelites were not strict monotheists; they were henotheists—recognizing many Gods, but serving only one. In the fourth century, Christian monotheism became the official religion of the late *Roman Empire, and for the past fifteen hundred years monotheism has remained the most popular religion in western culture—but polytheism is still very much alive around the world.

Polytheists, and some Christians, have difficulty with the claim that Christianity is monotheistic. The fourth-century Christian creeds, describing God as a "triune" deity (three-distinct-persons-yet-one-God), seem deliberately deceptive to polytheists and strict monotheists, like Jews and *Muslims. When modern Christians pray to the "second person of the *Trinity" (Jesus), or other "holy" figures, rather to than to God, radical monotheists are perplexed. An ancient Greek might wryly observe that such prayer signals a shift in power as happened among the Greek Gods, when *Cronus replaced his father *Uranus and was later deposed by his son, *Zeus.

Trinitarian Christians, however, emphatically deny that their faith is polytheistic and trace the Trinity, in particular, to the Gospel of John, although the evidence suggests that Christians were not consciously Trinitarian before the second or third centuries. Christians are asked to accept by faith the "mystery" of the Trinity; it cannot be rationally explained, we are told. In this regard a polytheist might observe that explaining multiple Gods is no more difficult than explaining one God consisting of three distinct individual deities. The appeal to "mystery" cuts both ways.

Nevertheless, in practice, monotheism has a distinct advantage. It is easier to practice than polytheism, for only "one" God must be obliged. Polytheists, on the other hand, must juggle homage to numerous Gods, each having a different personality and character. Since slighted Gods are easily offended, prudence dictates that the rites of several be satisfied.

What happened to all those ancient Gods? To claim they never existed is too simple. If one God exists, in principle several Gods can exist. My former History of Religions colleague used to say, "Gods are eternal and are still there, waiting to be rediscovered." Monotheists, of course, deny that they ever existed—and that may be true. But those who worshipped them were quite unlikely to be moved by such rhetoric, for they were as devout in their polytheistic faith as monotheists and Trinitarians are in theirs. The inutility of the Gods is fair warning: if even one God can become obsolete, all can.

⊰◇⊱

Some years ago I spent six hours on the Greek island of Delos climbing among the various sanctuaries and temples dedicated to the ancient Gods of the Greco-Roman world. Delos, a tiny island five kilometers by 1300 meters, began as a religious center dedicated to the *Ionian God *Apollo. Its influence in the *Cycladic islands endured from the seventh to the first centuries B.C.E. The devout of many faiths from all over the civilized world came to build their holy shrines on Delos, and for 600 years worshiped their Gods there. But now the site consists of crumbled ruins, whose white marble relics glisten like so many skeletons in the burning Greek sun. I wonder what happened to Apollo, *Asclepius, *Dionysus, *Isis, *Aphrodite, and the many other Gods of their generation? To my knowledge, today there is not a single active temple dedicated to the worship of these Gods, whose power captured the imagination of the ancient people of the Mediterranean world.

One modern response is to say: "They were not real Gods"—meaning that they never existed at all. However, I can just imagine the response of the hundreds of thousands who believed in them and through the years made their holy pilgrimages to Delos—just as modern Christians, Jews, and *Muslims make holy pilgrimage to their religious shrines today. The ancient believers came, offered prayers and sacrifices, and left inscriptions throughout the ancient world attesting to their healing at the power of these Gods. They would be shocked at the idea that Asclepius and Apollo were not "real." But today their sanctuaries are silent and these Gods considered historical artifacts.

What do we modern believers say about these silent sanctuaries of Delos? Do we say that these ancient Gods were not real or that they were simply products of the overactive imaginations of a primitive and superstitious people? Both explanations have been given, but neither is really satisfying. If such popular and influential Gods can so completely pass out of fashion, or be so easily dismissed as never existing, what should one think about one's own God? Is my faith really that different from these ancient faiths, whose Gods had as much power and influence in the ancient world as the Gods of current faiths enjoy in the modern world?

If there is no completely satisfactory answer to this question, it at least reminds us of the character of faith: faith is not demonstrable proof; it is only the evidence of a deeply held hope. God's existence cannot be quantitatively proven—at least not in a modern scientific test-tube sense. And that knowledge should make us all a little less arrogant in our own faith, and just a little more tolerant of the faiths of others.

5. SUPERSTITION, MAGIC, AND MODERN FAITH

Does modern Christian faith have its roots in ancient superstition? The answer, of course, depends on who you ask. Some years ago in an outdoor restaurant in Athens, Greece, an elderly gypsy woman persistently tried to sell me some tissues. Finally, she asked for a handout, but I refused even that. So she cursed me with inaudible mutterings and a left hand motion over my head. In the best Ozarks tradition, I immediately cursed her back with similar hand motions.

I don't think curses work—at least I was sure mine would not. And I was relatively sure hers would not, since I had been cursed, magnificently so, by a beggar some years earlier in a German restaurant with no ill effects. But since gypsy crones may be more effective than German beggars I admit to being a bit concerned at the time.

In Ozarks culture cursing is commonplace, but we don't seriously think our curses actually invoke the Powers of Darkness or Righteousness on someone's head. On the other hand, when we formally ask God to "bless" people or our projects, the more pious among us tend to presume that an official blessing by minister, rabbi, or priest confers something substantial on those who are blessed, as if God must honor the "blessing" given in his name—that God must "put his money where our mouth is," so to speak. We seem to regard "blessing" as performance language, rather than petition language. We say "God bless America," and think God actually does it—similar to what happens in Catholic Mass when bread and wine are transformed into the actual body and blood of Jesus when consecrated by the priest (you may not believe it so, but Roman Catholics do).

Do curses actually work? Do some among us have the ability to invoke Spiritual Powers to perform positive or negative acts? Perhaps; Jesus cursed the rich (Luke 6:24) and blessed the poor (Luke 6:20), for example, and Paul twice cursed those who disagreed with him (Galatians 1:8–9). And if Satan is a viable Force in the modern world, as many Christians seem to think, why couldn't the old gypsy's curse actually have worked on me?

It seems more likely, however, that cursing, blessing, and the evil eye are vestiges of humanity's primitive superstitious past. If you believe such things, they can affect you, not because of a curse's inherent power, but because of the power you give the curse. But you never know. So in Athens I poured a libation to the ancient Gods in hopes of mitigating the curse. It seemed appropriate. Since blessing and cursing seem to have been more effective in antiquity than today, perhaps the ancient Gods could better deal with such things. Curses, and the deflection of curses, are not part of modern faith—or are they? Does any Christian group practice cursing as a religious rite?

My brief brush with the dark powers raises the following issue: How much of our modern religious faith is ancient superstition? Superstition is defined as "the irrational belief that future events are influenced by specific behaviors lacking a casual relationship." In other words, the connection between cause and effect in superstition exists only in the minds of those who believe such things. Many people practice religion without knowing the reasons for their religious practices and beliefs, and—most important—whether the reasons for their behavior and belief make good sense. Shouldn't we be as critically discriminating in our religion as we are in the purchase of a new car?

⊰◈⊱

One area of common Christian practice that seems to relate to the relationship between faith and superstition is prayer. Does prayer work—like magic? Most people believe God answers prayer—even nonchurch folk. Generally, in all religions prayer is the invoking of greater than human powers to manipulate matters beyond the believer's control to induce a favorable outcome. In teaching his disciples to pray, Jesus gave them a model (Matthew 6:9-13). "Pray like this," he said, and in the prayer disciples are first taught to invoke the name of deity and then ritually present their petitions.

Ancient magic worked in a strikingly similar way: greater than human powers were invoked and ritual petition followed. In this way a *magus invoked supernatural powers to secure a desired outcome. So great is confidence in the ancient ritual, petition sometimes slips into solemn command: I adjure you (compare Matthew 26:63; Mark 5:7). Early Christians also used similar power language, solemnly invoking the name of Jesus to gain a desired result. For example, Peter is portrayed healing a lame man with the words: "in the name of Jesus Christ of Nazareth, walk" (Acts 3:6): invoking the name of Power enabled the petition (Mark 9:38; Acts 19:13-16)—just like magic.

Jesus himself did not perform mighty deeds in his own name, but is portrayed as authorizing the use of his name to facilitate petitions (John 14:13-14), since a name of Power produces the result. Many modern Christians still believe that *only* the name of Jesus will enable petitions (James 5:14-15)—just as ancient magicians manipulated human affairs by invoking the names of supernatural powers. In both cases it was believed that the prayer or magical rite was ineffective without the divine name and the ritual language.

Even Jesus was accused of performing mighty deeds by demonic powers (Mark 3:22), and oddly some of his healings were accomplished with magic-like gestures and words (Mark 7:3-35). He wore a "magic" garment bringing healing without his awareness (Mark 6:56) to people who touched it (Mark 5:25-29); and Paul performed healings by means of "magic" cloth (Acts 19:11-12), as others did through the agency of different powers (Acts 8:9-11).

Against the backdrop of ancient texts of ritual power, magic and prayer are cognates—the same kind of activity. The magician was as convinced in the efficacy of ritual magic as religious people are in the rite of prayer. Both believe their petitions tap the resources of greater than human power by which human affairs are manipulated. Both rituals invoke deity, employ ritual petition, and claim a mandated outcome

(Matthew 21:22), and as the existence of Christian magical texts attest, the line between Christian prayer and ancient magic is extremely fine. The similarity makes you wonder: if prayer works why not magic? Early Christians saw the problem and solved it by slandering the other powers and denying their effectiveness (2 Thessalonians 2:9–10), but not by denying their existence. Thinking we can finesse any God by words of ritual power, however, sounds suspiciously like *hubris—and that is something all Gods deplore.

⟁

Do black cats have anything to do with the Bible? The question is not as dumb as it first sounds. Faith and superstition, popularly regarded as completely opposite attitudes, are actually more closely related than most people imagine. The dictionary defines faith as "belief not based on proof," and superstition as "any blindly accepted belief or notion"; so some believers tend to think that people who "believe" the Bible have faith, but people who avoid black cats crossing their path are superstitious. But if you examine the definitions more closely, they are only distinguished by the negative word "blindly" characterizing superstition. Without it, superstition's definition works also for faith. Thus, one might conclude that superstition is belief lacking a reasonable basis and faith is belief enjoying a general respectability.

Can respectable "faith" be so easily distinguished from disreputable "superstition"? Put differently: is there a point when faith slips into superstition? For example, Paul describes the presence of angels in early Christian worship (1 Corinthians 11:10). For church folk, Paul is believable, but they dismiss as crass superstition the ancient Greek and Roman belief that nymphs and spirits inhabit certain sacred groves and springs. Why is belief in angels "faith" but belief in nymphs superstition?

Television evangelist *Robert Tilton frequently urged his audience to embrace their television sets while he prayed for their healing. Is that really different from the sick being healed and demons exorcized through objects taken from Paul's body and applied to persons so afflicted (Acts 19:11–12)? In Greco-Roman antiquity people generally believed that *Zeus had children by mating with human females. Modern church folk dismiss that as crass superstition and myth, but accept the divine birth of Jesus through Mary as historical fact. The author of James (5:14–15) believed the sick could be healed by anointing them with oil, and praying. How is that a legitimate item of faith, but the ancient belief that *Asclepius healed people who slept in his temples superstition? Oddly, in the middle first century the Romans described Christianity as a "pernicious superstition" (*Tacitus *Annals* 15.44), but accepted as a formal item of faith that *augurs could determine the will of the Gods by examining the entrails of sacrificed animals and observing the actions of sacred chickens.

Does superstition exist in modern religion? It depends on whom you ask. Baptists regard as "superstition" the Catholic belief that the bread and wine become the actual body and blood of Christ in the Mass. On the other hand, many Baptists believe that the words of the Bible are literally God's very own words—a view many Catholics regard, at best, as naïve and, at worst, irrational. Yet each group holds its own belief as a legitimate mystery of faith.

Aside from arrogance or *hubris, no consensus exists for distinguishing "responsible belief" from "irresponsible superstition." It appears to be a matter of personal perspective": "my belief is faith and yours, superstition." Distinguishing them generally hinges on who first uses the negative words most effectively and convincingly. But, of course, true believers won't need to rub a rabbit's foot to know the difference.

❖

What about visions, apparitions, and other divine visitations? Are such extrasensory experiences genuine? The answer has to be: maybe; it depends on who you talk to and how you view the world. In antiquity it was common knowledge that all Gods, including the Christian/Jewish God, communicated by means of visions. As the word suggests, a vision is "seen" in the mind's eye (so to speak). The ancients also saw apparitions, which, they claimed, were actually "something out there" that registered on their retinas. For example, Saul had the medium of Endor conjure up the spirit of the dead Israelite prophet, Samuel (1 Samuel 28:6–14). From these perspectives the resurrection "appearances" of Jesus in the gospels were either hallucinations (seen in the mind's eye) or apparitions (something out there). Both "experiences" were commonplace in antiquity and still persist in modern society: people still claim to see visions and apparitions. Dreams, however, are different. A dream is clearly something "seen" in the mind since the receiver is asleep. All the ancient Gods were thought to communicate through dreams, as did the Christian/Jewish God (see for example Matthew 1:20; 2:12, 13, 19).

The Greeks and Romans considered many things to be "visitations" or signs from the Gods. The flights of birds across certain quadrants of the sky portended success or failure. The Gods communicated through the entrails of animals, the croak of a raven, the song of a bird, or the fall of a tree across a road. Even the crowing of a rooster was thought to convey prophecies from the Gods, a view shared by the author of Mark's Gospel, where a crowing rooster confirms a prophecy of Jesus (Mark 14:30, 72).

We post-*Enlightenment moderns might well be skeptical of finding messages from the Gods or divine visitations in such natural occurrences, since it is in the nature of birds to sing and roosters to crow, whenever the notion strikes them. Nevertheless, ancient human beings conducted their lives on the basis of such commonplace occurrences they took to be divine messages—as well as the uncommon, such as an eclipse of the moon, or supposed astrological signs in the sky (like the star of Bethlehem, Matthew 2:2, 9–10). But at least with natural occurrences something material was available, so a dubious person could challenge the interpretation of the event, suggest a new one, or deny altogether that it was a sign.

But claims of seeing visions, apparitions, or communing with the deity "in spirit" are a different matter. There was nothing "material" to see (even apparitions are not technically "material"). Voices in the head, apparitions, visions, visitations, and dreams are impossible to verify. In such cases skepticism seems the better part of wisdom. The receiver may be absolutely certain of the experience, but for the rest of us there are other options to explain it: the "receiver" of the "divine message" may just be impressionable to suggestion, a charlatan, or emotionally disturbed. If there seems to be substance to the claim, the receiver may simply have misunderstood the "phenomena" (if such there were). Even the saints of old did not always "see" correctly, and hence entertained "angels unawares" (Hebrews 13:2). Perhaps God, for whatever reason, has deceived the receiver, as when the Jewish/Christian God sent lying spirits to deceive his own prophets (1 Kings 22:20–23). There is always the possibility that the receiver has been duped, not by the Gods, but by the forces of evil; for early Christians believed that Satan could transform himself into an "angel of light" (2 Corinthians 11:14). It is also entirely possible that purported receivers of such phenomena dupe themselves by wanting to "believe" something so strongly that they "see" or "hear" what they want. How can one with confidence objectively discriminate among these numerous possibilities for explaining claims of an extra-sensory experience?

The biggest problem, however, lies in the fact that receivers of supposed divine messages are limited by their humanity. The Gods may be perfect (or nearly so) but human beings are not. So the Gods may deliver their messages, but not even they can ensure that the message is accurately received, since overcoming a receiver's natural abilities would violate human "free will." The Gods may "speak" clearly enough, but we humans, by virtue of our humanity, always "hear" imperfectly. It must be so, since our spiritual leaders tell us different things on God's authority, and thereby we know their "free will" is fully operative and that the message is as much the purported receiver's as the God's. Even the Bible must be considered imperfect because the ancient "revelations" (if such they were) were communicated through receivers who were clearly conditioned by their ancient culture and society.

So how evaluate these claims of extra-sensory divine visitation? There is no way to be certain of the source of messages or visitations we think we receive. But if one assumes that God "is out there," or "hereabouts," or even communicating within us, the same caution and common sense we otherwise exercise in our daily lives is called for. Believing it to be so doesn't make it so!

6. DEATH AND DYING

I have always told my children that I intend to live forever, but time, the great enemy of us all, has set a mortal limit to our span of years and will eventually make a liar of me. We will all die. And what then? I have not thought much about that question—never seriously contemplating my own death. But early one morning, it forced itself on me. I awoke from a sound sleep in a clammy sweat, anxious, and profoundly disturbed, the sounds of the *Ionian Sea faint but distinct beyond the closed shutters of the room. My vaguely remembered dream replaying itself in my mind only increased my agitation. I had dreamed that the fabric of reality suddenly split down the side directly in front of me, and for a few seconds I stared into an empty void beyond. In the second I realized that absolutely nothing lay beyond, I knew my own personal mortality—not intellectually but viscerally. To a person my age the dream was scarcely a supernatural premonition. It was not a message from God, but rather a wakeup call from my own inner biological clock.

Religious faith, whether devout or nominal, deliberately pushes such thoughts from the mind—like *Scarlet O'Hara, we prefer to think about that kind of thing tomorrow. Religious faith, in fact, simply denies the void. But in that awful instant in my dream, all defenses down, I was forced to accept the void, the nonexistence that always surrounds everyone's immediate personal existence. In the final analysis, all we really know with complete certainty is what is, and sometimes we even get confused about that.

The dream did not drive me into depression. On the contrary, the next morning when the first rays of the sun spilled over the mountain, the air was fresher, the scent of the bougainvillea was sweeter, and bird-songs more enchanting. In short, after being confronted by the void in my dream, I realized that even a hangover is not without some merit. It is at least consciousness of a sort.

Religious faith insists that an essential "I" survives the inevitable leap into the void, and that some aspect of me survives the grave. Faith flatly denies that life is an ephemeral instance of existence surrounded by nothingness. The belief that "life" continues on the other side is a grand and courageous hope. For me, however, the other side is completely God's business. Living in the present, in spite of its troubles, disappointments, and all too frequent sufferings, remains a very certain and good thing. Life is the bird in the hand, so to speak. It should not be wasted on obsessive preoccupation with what exists, or does not, on the other side—a major concern of much modern religious faith. Nor should life be wasted in recriminations and a retreat from life that could lead to a premature leap into the void. The precious gift of consciousness is something to be cherished and nourished. "Wake up and sniff around for the roses," as my wife keeps telling me.

⋙◈⋘

The monuments, temples, and gravestones of ancient Greece, marble skeletons of a once living civilization, dot Greece's modern landscape, and clutter its museums. In Greece's heyday they were functional, facilitating access to the Gods. They testified to the people's faith, and to a keen sense of balance and beauty. Now they contribute to the country's economic base by luring travelers and capturing tourist dollars. Is that the ultimate value of ancient artifacts? Are such stones simply souvenirs of former civilizations, which modern society turns into profit ventures?

I suppose it depends on who visits them. For some, no doubt, the stones are just piles of rock impeding progress—a word by which we recent arrivals on the world scene render the past as somehow less significant in the light of the economic necessities of the present. But some years ago at the magnificent temple of *Poseidon in southern *Attica, I was struck differently. The temple was built in the fifth century B.C.E. in devotion to the Greek sea God Poseidon. It stands on a high promontory, near the edge of a steep cliff facing the open sea. Its gray-veined fluted columns, bone-like in the sun, are visible for miles to ships that pass below. Etched against a blue Grecian sky, it stands today as a reminder of the best qualities of the human spirit, and to the ancient Greek sense of symmetry and proportion. In some ways it attests the God-like nature of human beings, whose artifacts bring order to nature's randomness, as God brought order to chaos in the act of creation. These symmetrical products of human hands bring striking regularity into nature's casual course. Straight lines are a human invention; Mother Nature doesn't make them.

But these stone vestiges of the Greek past also remind us that we humans vanish as rapidly as wreaths of smoke from a dry cheap cigar. Just maybe the name recognition of the more famous will last a bit longer. But not even our greatest will last forever. One day when our own culture is a vague memory among our posterity, even the great names and their deeds will be lost. For example, the name of the *Spartan general, *Leonidas, today is no longer a household word, but his courageous stand at *Thermopylae in 480 B.C.E., at the cost of his own life and the lives of his soldiers, directly contributed to the preservation of Greek culture and the rise of western civilization.

These Greek stones also remind me that our own gravestones, monuments, and majestic skyscrapers, now a part of a thriving culture, are like those of ancient Greece, and eventually destined for obsolescence. Neither the ancient Greek stones, nor our own, will endure forever, for not even stones are impervious to wind and rain. Eventually inscriptions fade, and then the stones themselves weather and disintegrate.

In the final analysis, men are not Gods, and all the generous offerings of their hands to the Gods, their monuments, gravestones, and temples, like their own bleached bones, are so much hay and stubble disappearing in the wind. If there is a single lesson to be learned from Poseidon's temple, the moral is in the stones: make the most of your three minutes in the sun.

⸙❖⸙

If honest, adults resent aging and cling to youth as long as they can. We even conceal the early stages of aging describing it as "growing up," though no adequate euphemism exists for the far end of life. Seven decades (or so) of life seem awfully short! About the time we become comfortable with ourselves, we are past the point of engaging life—or so our children and grandchildren suggest. For example, Telly owns an Internet café on the Greek island of Paros in the *Cyclades. His eighty-year old father had a stroke while preparing for market a string of *Octopodi, caught in a full day's fishing. Forty-year old Telly is frustrated that his father, now confined to the house, does not understand that eighty-year olds simply cannot continue life as usual. Father, however, insisted on doing what had always given his life meaning, and was willing to trade longevity for quality, which he apparently construed as continued life engagement. Telly sees life from its middle, and father from the far end.

Aging is a bitch! No other word will do. We do not "grow old gracefully." On the far end, things go wrong with the human frame, even when we enjoy reasonably good health. For one thing, skin wrinkles and sags in an odd sort of way. A diminution of the life force frustrates, but most learn to cope with living in death's shadow.

Many view aging and death theologically—were it not for Adam's "sin," Paul insists, death would not have entered the world (Romans 5:12). And so we, being sinners, must all die. From this perspective, humanity was originally created for infinite living, but lost that capacity because of sin. The inevitable death sentence may be somewhat delayed, however, for the Bible promises long life to the righteous (Proverbs 16:31; 1 Kings 3:14) and associates premature death with sin (Ezekiel 33:10–16). The Bible even gives examples of incredibly long lives—for example, Methuselah lived 969 years (Genesis 5:27). Even as a naïve Baptist youth, I knew people could not live that long. And the idea that God ends a person's life because of "unrighteousness" is denied by human experience, as even the Bible realizes (Ecclesiastes 7:15): the righteous do die young and the wicked live full long lives. Single perspective explanations, such as Genesis 3:17–19 (Adam's willful disobedience in *Eden), cannot do full justice to the complexity of the human situation. Aging and obsolescence are simply the way things work in our world. We all age, if fortunate enough. Aging well (if there is such a thing) and long life have little to do with religious piety, and much to do with genetics, diet, exercise, and a determined mental attitude.

Aging and death are inevitable under either rationale. So what truly matters is how we handle aging and confront our own demise. Do we throw in the towel and become spectators? Or do we continue pushing our limits and engaging life beyond the property line? Dylan Thomas, the Welsh poet, answered it this way: "Do not go gentle into that good night,/ Old age should burn and rave at close of day;/ Rage, rage against the dying of the light."

⊸◈⊶

Why then do many die young, some live with dementia into old age, and others are blessed with long life, and good health? It is not a question that can be answered definitively, but many try. The ancient Greeks attributed it to Fate, or *Kismet—a blind inevitable Force determining human destiny, in which many still believe. By far the most popular answer in Christianity, however, is that God alone determines our prosperity, length of life, and the state of our health. Many soldiers have said it this way: "God gave me a second chance to live."

If our lives are contingent on God's will, or Fate, we all can stop worrying, for then none of us has any control over the length or quality of life. Our future is set. With a quick roll of the dice blind Fate determines our lot! Likewise, if God determines our destiny, life cannot be extended by diet or medication. But if God decides otherwise, our lives will be long and healthy, whether we give up fatty foods and count calories, or not. Candidly, most don't really believe that God alone determines length and quality of life. We profess to believe our religious professionals when they assure us God has planned our lives—but we are not confident enough to ignore our physician's advice. Even people of faith buy medical insurance! By exercise, diet, and pills devout Christians, *Muslims, Jews, and others aim to extend both quality and length of life—which is a kind of denial that God is in absolute control. It does not seem reasonable to blame God for our health—the state of our arteries, for example. Why would God, who was apparently unconcerned about the thousands who died in the *tsunami in Indonesia in 2004, concern himself with my arteries and high cholesterol?

Apparently what we actually mean by the confession that God alone determines life's outcomes is "God helps those who help themselves." So we listen to our doctors, change our diet, and exercise to improve and prolong life. Maybe we can extend life, but not always. Take the case of

Terri Schiavo. She suddenly collapsed in her home in 1990. One minute she was young and healthy and the next she was comatose. She "lived" in a persistent vegetative state until 2005, and died shortly after her artificial life support was removed. Her physicians kept her "alive," and the courts "decided" the day of her death.

If human destiny and health are inevitably predetermined by God or blind Fate, why should we even try to improve our situation in life? The answer is because we can! Though they are not always successful, physicians have documented time and again cases of improved health and longer lives for persons who would have died much sooner, except for medical intervention. Apparently, neither Fate nor God has absolute control over human life in the modern world—unless we consider physicians as God's emissaries, or the envoys of Fate.

We find great comfort in the idea that each of us fits some way into a universal grand master plan—in spite of the randomness we see about us. The answer best fitting our human condition, however, is this: health and life span are determined by good genes, a little bit of luck—and a smart physician. Why shouldn't that knowledge comfort us as well? No question but that we humans are term-limited in life, but our "lot" is not predetermined. What we do between birth and death is up to us. While praying may or may not help, it shouldn't hurt, but an unhealthy diet and lack of exercise will definitely be detrimental to your health—no matter how good your genes are.

❦

My wife keeps telling me to relax and learn to smell the roses. But I have noticed that she is as preoccupied with her law practice as she finds me to be with my writing. We human beings are always so busy about many things. Some years ago my mother had surgery—the big C. But the surgeons were optimistic that an operation would get all of the cancer. Mother called all her children together and insisted—insisted—they be present for the surgery. This was the first time the entire family had been together in one place, at one time, in more than twenty years.

There were good reasons why we were not able to be together during those twenty years. But mother's insistence caused us all to rearrange schedules, revise priorities, and be present on the day she entered the hospital. The physician told us the surgery was an unqualified success. He got all the cancer and indeed, as it turned out, mother's circulation briefly improved. She had complained about poor circulation in her legs for two years. In the recovery room, however, she had a stroke; she was paralyzed on her right side and lost her speech capability. The first day she could squeeze hands and seemed to be aware of people about her—though I was never really sure she recognized me as me. But we were grateful she was alive.

The next day she had another stroke and it rendered her comatose. For more than a week, most of the family was present, hoping for a miracle, believing in miracles, praying for a miracle, but in the back of my mind I realized that for every miracle there were thousands or more non-miracles. Mother did not want to be placed on extended life support. But when the physicians presented us with the decision whether or not to put her on a feeding tube, we were not able to deny Mother the tubes that brought food and liquids. We waited around for eight or nine days and then slowly drifted away to return to those business affairs that occupy most of our waking hours.

And then the physician gave us another ultimatum. We must decide on a permanent attachment in her stomach to accommodate a feeding tube. With much agony, we decided against it, because we could not consign her to years of vegetable-like existence. It was not an easy decision. So we rearranged priorities again, and the family gathered in the hospital room to wait for Mother to die.

Alone in my car on the seven-hour drive back to Clarksville, Tennessee, I wondered why we human beings can so easily revise priorities at the time of death, why we can relegate all of our important activities and responsibilities to a second level when a family member is near death or dies, but cannot seem to do it when they were alive, when we could enjoy each other's company. It is odd, isn't it, that a person's dying is given higher priority than a person's living.

Mother would have been pleased that her children had gotten reacquainted after all those years apart, that we had spent so much time visiting over the phone and in person over the last month leading up to her death. Her dying did what her living apparently could not—it brought the family together. But I imagined that it probably wouldn't last, because each of us had busy lives in different parts of the country—and many "important" things to do.

Mother was a great lady, and the memory of her smile will outlast the memory of her dying. She deserves to be remembered. At the time I thought I would plant a red rosebush in her memory, red for the vibrant life she enjoyed so much—if I could find the time. I never did.

⋖◇⋗

In the pale gray between dark and the uncanny Greek dawn alone in my thoughts trying to go back to sleep, I was struck (and still am) by how utterly and absolutely alone we are. Every individual's situation mirrors the circumstance of humanity. We are, so far as we know, utterly and absolutely alone in the universe. I find myself trapped inside a body I simply do not recognize anymore—gray hair, assorted pains, and flaccid skin. Who is this stranger whose body I inhabit utterly alone?

We live alone and we die alone. Even though we share a lifetime of joy and sadness, hope and disappointment, with family and close friends, in the still hours of the morning we know profound solitude. No one really knows what we think, or precisely what motivates us to move the bodies we inhabit to laughter or tears. We find difficulty in expressing our deepest feelings—the spoken word always falling short of what goes on inside.

A few years ago, watching my sister's life dribble away from an unconscionable cancer, I realized what the final moments would be like for each of us. Although family was always there by her side and friends came to visit, she was still very much alone. How could we be "with her"? Her body wasted away and only she could deal with it; we watched and suffered, but the pain was all her own. No words seemed weighty enough to comfort either her or us. Even the well-meaning words of the religious professionals seemed inadequate, their sincere prayers rang hollow in my ears. We were by her side; yet at the end only she lived inside the failing body alone, in her thoughts with her faith, facing dying alone—like each of us suddenly awake in the gray hours between the dark and the dawn alone in our thoughts.

At some point in our journey we all will experience the terrible solitude in the last minutes—alone with only our faith, perhaps in a momentary flash of regret considering a life that forked little lightening, but certainly pondering "What's next?" All of us have some kind of faith—an idea of our place in the universe: the apple of God's eye perhaps, or simply dust from the stars returning whence it came. In either case, besides the pain, faith is all there is in the gathering dusk between bright consciousness and the dark side. We can only hope the faith that sustained our living will endure our dying.

It was like that for Jesus of Nazareth as well. Mark is the earliest writer to describe his dying. Mark's information had been passed down orally for a generation, so he was not an eyewitness; at least Christians in the second century did not think he was. But Mark's narrative has clearly captured Jesus' death as a human experience. He portrays Jesus in the final moments alone with his faith praying: "My God, my God, why have you forsaken me?" (Mark 15:34). His women friends and acquaintances watched from afar, but they were not really "with him;" how could they be? He died in the darkness toward the end of the day, as one of us, utterly alone with his faith.

At *Delphi above the entrance to the temple of the Greek God *Apollo was inscribed the maxim "Know thyself." It sounds like sage advice for the end of the day.

✧

We will all die—the only questions are how soon and how we will be remembered.

The issue of dying came up one day in the middle of my daily three-mile "run" with my jogging cronies from the Missouri State University history department. I don't know if it was due to our sharing a sense of the vicissitudes of history, or if it had to do with us getting older, grayer, and paunchier, perhaps both. Someone in the group wondered about the value of the esoteric research we academic types produce. "Few people read it" was the consensus; so "What is its value?" was the question. I quickly responded, "We do it because it's interesting. If we don't find it interesting, we shouldn't do it."

On reflection, I clearly spoke too quickly. We all have to do things we don't find particularly interesting. Life being what it is one simply cannot avoid boring and uninteresting moments. But it set me to thinking about the quality and value of my life in terms of the long sweep of eternity. When I feel those cold fingers reaching up from my ankles, how will I evaluate my life? In those last few minutes (if minutes there be) that my life rushes before my eyes, how will I evaluate it?

I cannot, of course, be certain that my views will not change in my dotage; they have changed over the years. But if I were asked that question on that particular day, my reply would be that there are three ways I think I would assess my life: (a) Did I do interesting things? (b) Did I contribute to the happiness and welfare of others? (c) Did I do everything I always intended to do? If I can answer these three questions affirmatively, I will depart with few regrets.

At the time, I did wonder why my three criteria were not more religious, since I consider myself a religious person. I finally decided that so much religious language sounds pompous, if not downright arrogant. (It is possible that I am here confusing the message with the messenger.) Religious language is a serious attempt to address our common human condition, but it simply doesn't wear well in the eight-to-five world. Much religious language is like a Sunday-go-to-meeting suit, which is inappropriate for the jobs that most of us do Monday through Saturday.

Religious concepts, however, may well be appropriate. But enduring religious concepts should be expressible in eight-to-five language, as is the case with the stories Jesus told. The parables use the sweaty language of first-century *Palestinian village life.

I could likely easily have "baptized" my three criteria saying them more religiously. But dying seems like a time for simple and unambiguous language. One ought to be able to die comfortably in the honest, earthy discourse of everyday life.

7. HOLY DAYS AND RELIGIOUS FEASTS

Christmas in America has something for virtually everyone—even the Scrooges, and particularly the *Bob Cratchits. Ancient customs (Christian and non-Christian) and diverse modern traditions have become so mingled, it is difficult to know what it all means, if anything. Christmas in the marketplace now begins before Thanksgiving and ends sometime after the beginning of the New Year (or whenever you take down your Christmas tree). Merchants capitalize on every trapping of Christmas from Rudolph to the crèche, and music serenading your shopping ranges from "Jingle Bells" to "Away in a Manger." Christmas marketing is highly successful, and at this time of year we are in a mood to be separated from our money—whether giving gifts, or responding to some obscure charity making its appeal after our second trip to the *wassail bowl. Commercialism is not all bad, however. In many ways, what is good for the marketplace is good for the country, and what is good for the country generally translates into chickens in our Christmas pots.

The season has religious roots as well—a lot of different roots, it seems. Naturally we are reminded of the baby born in Bethlehem (or was it really Nazareth?). But before Christians started celebrating the birth of Jesus, in late December the *Roman Empire had long celebrated *Saturnalia, a Roman agricultural festival incorporating many of the same customs we still observe at Christmas. *Saturn was a venerable deity in Italy fabled to have reigned during a period of peace and happiness. The twenty-fifth of December (then reckoned as the winter *solstice) was celebrated both as the birth of the *Invincible Sun, and *Mithras, the Persian deity of light. The ancient Jewish Feast of Hanukkah, the Festival of Lights, which commemorates the rededication of the Jewish Temple and Jewish political independence, also falls in December. The customs and symbols of these non-Christian festivals have merged with the Christian, and continue to be celebrated in the American winter solstice: lights, candles, gift-giving, family gatherings, shopping, evergreen trees, and garnishes of holly and mistletoe. Somehow it all seems to make sense even to largely Christian America. There is something distinctly egalitarian and democratic about our solstice. The "huddled masses" brought their winter customs with them, and we later generations have woven them all (*menorah, *piñata, wassail bowl, parties, Santa Claus, Christmas trees, midnight masses, and *Yule logs) into a textured solstice tapestry.

I like the diversity—even its commercialism. It all enriches the texture. But it is difficult to know how it all fits together. What does it all mean? We celebrate both the religious and the secular aspects of Christmas. We are nostalgic when Bing Crosby sings "White Christmas," and enjoy the cycle of parties and receptions with their tinsel, lights, foodstuffs, and spirits (hopefully, in moderation). On the other hand, the sobering thought that some two thousand years ago the secular was uniquely invaded by the holy, as Christian faith affirms it, still encourages hope in even the most skeptical Scrooge.

Making sense of this collage of diverse symbols and customs in its entirety, and finding some significant reason for the season as we now celebrate it, however, is a challenge. Of course, some people have all the answers and dismiss everything except the lights at the end of their own myopic tunnels. I prefer to try to embrace it all. In my more reflective moments I see the American solstice symbolizing a search for stability and happiness. In the confusion and uncertainty seemingly dominating the world around us, these mingled traditions serve as anchors. We return to them annually because they are familiar and comforting. They nourish a deep-seated hope in western culture, best expressed for me by the ancient Jewish longing for the advent of an ideal ruler, whose eternal reign is characterized by peace, justice, and righteousness (Isaiah 9:7). This is a hope shared by all people of goodwill, and well worth celebrating.

The message of the first Christmas has endured for almost two thousand years, surviving: translation from ancient into modern culture, the attacks of hostile rationalists, the naiveté of biblical literalists, its crass commercialism in the marketplace, the self-serving interests of overzealous pietists, and its amalgamation with other competitive holiday traditions through the centuries.

The story of the birth of Jesus has continued to capture the imagination of the most creative and able talent of western culture. Under its influence artists have produced many of the masterpieces of our Judeo-Christian heritage. And today, at the beginning of the twenty-first century, we are still influenced by it. Motivated by the ancient Christmas story, we moderns have been led to acts of altruism, self-sacrifice, and charity that surprise even us. It is difficult to react with a bah-humbug attitude when we are bombarded with so much Christmas "magic" at that time of year. There is a grandeur, a nobility, associated with Christmas that stirs the slumbering chords of the highest human ideals. For that reason, the "Christmas story" is authentic in a way that historical criticism cannot confirm, or even investigate.

Why do these narratives describing Jesus' birth still speak to modern human beings? It is not because of their unity, philosophical sophistication, or technical excellence. For example, there are actually two different Christmas stories in the New Testament, one by Matthew and another by Luke. Mark and John either do not know a birth narrative, or simply do not report what they know. (They make similar points about Jesus in other ways.) And many modern, even devout, church people have confided that they have difficulty accepting the credibility of miraculous elements in the narratives—virgin birth, angels, star that led the wise men, etc. For many, these are serious obstacles to faith, except for the "true believer," who makes believing them the test of true faith. Such miraculous elements, however, are common in the literature of antiquity, where they are used to validate the careers of great men. Compare, for instance, birth stories about *Asclepius, *Hercules, and *Alexander the Great. The real "miracle" of Christmas, however, lies elsewhere: in how it inspires us to treat one another, for example.

The Christmas narratives remain relevant in our day, in spite of their legendary and mythical character. Each narrative expresses the deepest longing and noblest aspiration of the human spirit. Their vision rises above those insignificant borders separating denominations and even religions. They address two basic issues that concern our common human family, regardless of heritage or creed. All of us want to believe that what they proclaim is capable of realization in human life: they speak to our awareness of human finitude—our terrible dread of the infinite, however we label it; and they address our very deep human desire for peace in the world at all levels of human existence (Luke 1:76–79).

Matthew proclaims that the humanity of a particular Jewish child born in a remote village of the *Roman Empire, in a naive and prescientific age, brings a gracious God near to all human beings (Matthew 1:21–23): the message is infinity need not be feared! Luke holds forth this event as a promise of "peace on earth" (Luke 2:14). The possibility of being free from the terror of our finitude and of finding peace in a turbulent and frequently brutal world is "good news" indeed. Such hope brings comfort to every human heart, and is worthy of celebration by all of us.

❦

There is an undeniable magic in the Christmas season, but Christmas day by itself does not always live up to our expectations. In short, our preparations are often more exciting than what we actually do on Christmas day. Leading up to Christmas, the days are alive with excitement and cheer; a festive mood, reflected in the variegated lights of city streets and private homes, even invades the usually sterile workplace.

On the other hand, after the brief excitement of waking up to Santa Claus on Christmas morning, and the opening of gifts that leave the room knee-deep in wrapping paper, Christmas day for adults is usually quiet, undisturbed and almost dull.

In some ways, Christmas day is similar to a rum cake. There are more "spirits" in the preparation. When baked, the cake, like the day, retains the taste of the rum, but the "spirit" has lost its punch—hence the question: What is really special about Christmas? Many of our Christmas traditions did not originate as early Christian traditions. Mistletoe, for example, played a significant role in the ancient *Celtic religion. The Roman celebration of *Saturnalia, December 17–23, included the giving of gifts and the lighting of candles. Even December 25 was first celebrated in the ancient world as the birthday of *sol invictus and *Mithras, the Persian God of light, whose mysteries competed with Christianity in the second and third centuries.

The earliest Christians did not originally celebrate the birth of Jesus as a special day. The Gospels of Mark and John are able to describe who Jesus was without birth narratives. Aside from Easter and *Pentecost, early Christians celebrated *Epiphany on the sixth of January, which originally was a celebration of Jesus' baptism as his public manifestation to the world as the Son of God. It was not until the middle of the fourth century that December 25 was appropriated by Christians as a special day to celebrate Jesus' birth.

What Americans do at Christmas does not really appear to be a religious celebration. We observe the season and the day and link them with the birth of Jesus, but the real emphasis in America is on gift giving and family gatherings rather than on religious celebrations. For example, when Christmas falls on Sunday, as it did in 1994, many churches tend to reduce the regularly scheduled Sunday activities, rather than making religious capital on the convergence of Sunday with Christmas day.

These observations are not intended as a criticism of modern Christmas practices. I particularly enjoy the commercialism of the season. Perhaps it is because I have spent too many Christmas seasons in countries where the major religion is not Christian. As a result, I have come to think of our Christmas celebration as an assimilation of American culture to Christian faith. Or put in theological language: For good or ill, Christmas represents a secular symbolical incarnation of Christ in American culture. In the trappings of our Christmas celebration, I find little that is uniquely Christian. And yet, after having said all of this, I do find something very different and special in the Christmas celebration. At Christmas time the very air is charged with a sense of expectation, joy, hope, and goodwill. Except for Easter, I can think of no other day in our national festive calendar that unites nations and peoples throughout the world. If Jesus had done no more than give his name to a day that brings families together and inspires the celebration of those noblest aspects of our human character—love, joy, hope, goodwill, benevolence, generosity, and peace—it would have been a marvelous gift to humankind. One might even say, "A divine gift."

If those who wrote the Bible had thought like modern believers, no disagreements would be found in the Bible to astonish modern readers. Take the simple question, *Did Jesus give a "sign" to identify himself as Son of God?* The early Christian gospels do not agree on the answer. Mark represents Jesus refusing to give a sign (Mark 8:11–12). In Matthew and Luke, on the other hand, he did give a sign—"The sign of Jonah" (Matthew 12:38–39; 16:1–4; Luke 11:29), but the interpretations of what the sign of Jonah meant are different (Matt 12:40–42; Luke 11:30–32). In the Gospel of John, on the other hand, virtually everything Jesus did was a sign revealing his glory (for instance, John 2:1–11).

What is a sign, anyway? The ancient Mediterranean people considered a "sign" a visible indicator of some hidden purpose of the Gods. They regarded extraordinary, and even ordinary, occurrences as signs, or messages, from the Gods. The Roman writer *Cicero wrote an essay, describing "signs" as one way the Gods communicated with people, and noted even the songs and flights of birds as among the most infallible of signs, or omens.

Matthew, Mark, and Luke label few things as signs. John, on the other hand, labels virtually everything Jesus does as a sign. One odd sign, only in Luke, relates to the birth of Jesus. An angel tells the shepherds watching over their flocks in the fields that a savior is born to them in the Judean village of Bethlehem. This savior is the Jewish Messiah—the Lord (Luke 2:11). The sign they are given is "a new born child wrapped in baby clothes lying in a manger" (2:12). As signs go, this has to be one of the most common, ranking alongside those things the Romans found significant—a tree falling in the forest, a random flight of birds, and the croaking of a raven. Astonishingly ordinary, it lacks all trappings of majesty and royalty. Why not use Matthew's star in the east—or the heavenly choir making the announcement to the shepherds? These would be signs worthy of a divine birth! Why pick such humble circumstances in a backward land in a country village on the edge of the *Roman Empire? Luke doesn't even appeal to biblical prophecy to account for the ordinariness of the event.

The sign would scarcely help the shepherds recognize the child, but discloses the hidden purposes of God, as Luke understood them.

Considering the circumstances, the sign indicates that God's Messiah, and Lord, has become one of us—a homespun man of the people. He is not a king, or divinity, at least not in the usual sense. His birth lacks all the expected fanfare associated with royalty. A theologian might explain Luke's sign as: the God "out there" (the transcendent) has drawn near (is immanent). The implications are staggering: the divine is no longer mediated through ritual, pomp, ceremony, and mystery, but is accessible in the ordinary things of common human experience. In short, the Christmas story is about the humanizing of God, rather than the divinizing of humanity. In Matthew, Jesus associates himself with "the least of those in the human family" like this: "I was hungry and you gave me food, I was thirsty and you gave me drink, I was a stranger and you welcomed me, I was naked and you clothed me, I was sick and you visited me, I was in prison and you came to me" (Matthew 25:34–37). In other words, God is found "with us," particularly with the least member of the human family (Matthew 25:37–40, 42–45). Luke's concept of the *significance* of Christmas is profoundly sobering, and could potentially change all our lives, by changing how we see and treat others—and surely that is a hope worth celebrating.

⊰◈⊱

Easter is the holiest day in the Christian calendar, linking Christians of all confessions across the world. For believers, Jesus' resurrection is prelude and promise of their own resurrection. But his resurrection was not a "historical" event—at least, not in the same sense that his crucifixion was. Many were crucified in antiquity, and, hence, crucifixion is the same kind of human event as the dedication of a new university building, or a car wreck at a major intersection. For modern historians, these things happen in a sense that Jesus' resurrection did not. The resurrection belongs to what Christian theologians dub "salvation history"—the "record" of God's saving acts. For Christian theologians, the resurrection climaxes these saving acts. But salvation history is not *human* history, or even what secular historians consider "history." The resurrection of Jesus plays a significant role in ecclesiastical histories, but is not treated as historical event in modern textbooks of the history of western civilization.

All religions have a "salvation history" in which Gods are portrayed acting in human affairs. The resurrection of Jesus is that kind of extraordinary event. Thus, the resurrection of Jesus is as much history as the resurrection of the *Pythagorean philosopher *Apollonius, whose followers claimed to experience his presence after his death in the first century.

Not all ancient believers understood Jesus' resurrection the same. The gospels depict an empty tomb, suggesting that Jesus was physically resuscitated, leading modern Christians to interpret their own resurrection as physical resuscitation. But Paul, who wrote earlier than the gospels, specifically excluded this possibility (1 Corinthians 15:35–57). Paul believed God had "raised," not resuscitated, Jesus, and described his resurrection as a "spiritual event": "flesh and blood cannot inherit the kingdom of God" (1 Corinthians 15:50), Paul said—and this holds true for all believers. Alas, Paul never explained the meaning of the "spiritual body" of Jesus. But Christians who expect to be physically *resuscitated* after dying do not share Paul's hope.

Many believe resurrection can be described in other than the materialistic language of physical resuscitation. For them, the empty tomb is an affirmation that God controls the world, despite evidence to the contrary. Believing in resurrection is a way of talking about life and the meaningfulness of life in the face of death. Affirming resurrection is a way of denying that life is a tiny raft of existence awash in a sea of nothingness. Nontraditional believers celebrate the resurrection of Jesus as God's affirmation of humanity. As Claude in the sixties rock musical "Hair" said: "I believe in God and I believe that God believes in Claude, that's me, Claude Hooper Bukowski." In these and other ways nontraditional faith affirms, and celebrates, confidence that the creator is not finished with his creature.

Nontraditional ways of understanding Christian belief may not seem tangible enough for some, but they are as tangible as Paul's explanation of resurrection as a "spiritual" event. Both Paul's view, and secular faith alluded to above, are ways of affirming the resurrection of Jesus, and qualifying for God's future—whatever that may be. They share strong faith in God and courageous hope for the future. And, after all, even Paul described his own faith, and future expectations, as "hope" (1 Corinthians 15:19). In our moments of truth, we all do.

8. POSTSCRIPT: REASON AND FAITH

Reading back through these essays, I see them written by someone who stands on the border between faith and reason, trying to respect the old traditions, but recognizing that human reason, which has accomplished so much in the sciences, must be honored in the religious life as well. Faith, a trust or confidence not based on proof, is a personal attitude absolutely essential to human life. Our society could not function without it; faith is essential for the well-being of family and other human relationships. For instance, parents have faith that children will exercise good judgment when they are out in the community without parental supervision. Sometimes, however, that faith is misplaced and children misbehave. Under such conditions hopefully reason will trump faith and the parents will impose stronger controls on their children.

Before the advent of modern business practices, contracts and other agreements were sealed with only a handshake. Such negotiations operated on the premise that "a man's word was his bond," meaning that in verbal contracts each had faith the other would fulfill the negotiated agreement, even though nothing existed to prove an agreement had ever even been made. People who negotiated in "bad faith," and did not keep their word, found that others would not make agreements with them—even people who had never had a contract with them before. Thus the attitude of faith in human relationships and joint endeavors is modified and shaped by both personal experience and reason—in this situation reason is the mental ability to form judgments, draw conclusions, and make inferences based on data completely apart from personal experience.

Today in virtually every area of life, except one, the exercise of faith is always conditioned by human reason. For example, we don't loan money to people who have a reputation of not meeting their obligations, because we reasonably conclude there is a strong probability they will not repay the loan. We don't unconditionally trust those who deceive us, because we reasonably conclude a good likelihood exists that we will be deceived again. "Fool me once, shame on you; fool me twice shame on me" is the attitude. Only in the area of personal religious belief has faith generally not been conditioned by human reason.

The struggle between faith and reason, or perhaps better, the struggle between religion and science has been going on since the *Renaissance, a term given to the revival of learning that spread across Europe in the fourteenth through the seventeenth centuries. It was a period of the rediscovery of the art, literature, and science of classical Greece and Rome. The energies of an educated person in this period were redirected from the world of the spirit to the physical world—from theological reflection to curiosity about humankind and the natural world. Humanism, not spiritualism, marked the "spirit" of the Renaissance Age.

The struggle has not gone well for religion. The ancient dogmas of the church, one after another, have fallen before the steady progression of human science. Human beings aided by reason and the scientific method have been cracking the "genetic code" of the universe and providing answers to questions that once were considered the exclusive purview of religion. Today every schoolchild not educated in a school that gives priority in education to religious confessions knows that some ancient dogmas are not true: the earth is neither flat nor the center of the universe, disease is not caused by sin, and human beings were not created in a single moment of time but evolved from lower forms of life. Human science has created life in a petri dish, taken us to the moon, transplanted human hearts, cloned animals, and begun the exploration of the universe. The control of traditional religion on the human mind is under fire as never before in human history.

In 1930, H. L. Mencken wrote:

> The truth is that every priest who really understands the nature of his business is well aware that science is its natural and implacable

enemy. He knows that every time the bounds of exact knowledge are widened, however modestly, the domain of theology is correspondingly narrowed. If Christian divines admit today that the world is round and revolves around the sun, it is only because they can't help themselves—because the fact has been so incontrovertibly proven that even the mob has had to accept it. So long as they could do so safely they denounced it bitterly, and launched their most blistering anathemas upon those who defended it. In precisely the same way they opposed, while they could, every other advance in knowledge, not only in the physical sciences but in philosophy and mathematics.[1]

Looking back over the past one hundred years, I would have to say: Mencken was both right and wrong. Science is not religion's natural enemy, but human science is clearly the chief enemy to any faith that rejects the moderating role of human reason in every area of life—including religion.

In long term, if religious faith is to survive in the modern world it must begin its confession with the dictum, "Faith may not require me to believe what I find to be patently false." The struggle in the first century between competing factions tracing their origins in some way to Jesus of Nazareth has remained typical of Christian faith through the intervening years: each first-century group was searching for what made sense from their inherited traditions. In spite of the *Orthodox creeds that have largely typified modern Christianity since the fourth and fifth centuries of the Common Era, that situation has not changed: In every generation it has been necessary for people of faith to search for new ways to make sense of their faith. The standard creeds of the church are clearly not a once and for all time statement of faith but merely one ancient attempt to clarify the nature of faith at a particular point in time.[2] The problem has always been how to keep faith with the ancient traditions while keeping pace with the acquisition of human knowledge.

Today the Bible has become a major block to resolving the tension between faith and reason. In American religion the Bible has become an icon—a sacred object of veneration. As an icon, it is not considered a fit subject for "criticism," though up to a point it may be gently "analyzed." In the popular mind the Bible constitutes the ultimate revelation of God to humankind; principally it is meant to be studied, and its moral teaching and religious principles implemented in individual lives and throughout society. Reason, on the other hand, is naturally curious about everything in the world. In the spirit of the *Renaissance, reason's scientific spirit considers everything subject to criticism, analysis, and challenge; nothing is exempt—and particularly not the Bible.

Since the *Enlightenment (beginning of the age of reason) of the late seventeenth and eighteenth centuries, human reason has applied itself to the Bible. This period began the modern critical study of the Bible, and the results of three hundred years of biblical criticism have demonstrated beyond any question that the Bible is a human product with a past. The Bible's rediscovery as a text subject to the vicissitudes of human history has clearly undermined faith in the Bible as iconic object. The Bible was the one anchor of certainty left to the church after the *Protestant Reformation. No longer did the church have the authoritative pronouncements of the Roman Catholic Pope speaking truth from God in the areas of faith and morals; the watchword of the Protestant Reformation was *sola scriptura.* "Scripture alone" was the guide for religious faith and practice according to the reformers. The Roman Catholic Church subordinated the Bible to the church, noting that it was the church that had produced the Bible, and thus the church has sole authority to interpret it. The protestant reformers, on the other hand, subordinated the church to the Bible, and made "Scripture alone" (*sola scriptura*) authoritative for the church. The Enlightenment, however, subordinated the church, the Bible, and religion in general, to human reason, and in so doing discredited both church and Bible as the authoritative voice of God in the modern world. Human beings were left to face God alone without the security net of either the church or the Bible. Since the Enlightenment, reason increasingly trumps revelation.

With only human reason and ancient tradition as a general guide, we followers of Jesus today are left to "work out our salvation with fear and trembling," as Paul put it (Philippians 2:12). At some point, those who think for themselves will be confronted by the clash between reason and traditional faith. At that point begins the restructuring of faith, because reason is a bully and will not allow a rational person mindlessly to repeat ancient confessions that make little sense in the modern world. The essays in this book to a great extent chronicle my own struggle between personal faith and reason.[3]

ENDNOTES

Introduction

1. Jewish Chaplains were only commissioned as late as 1918, but apparently were not effectively a part of the system until World War II; see Earl F. Stover, *Up From Handymen: The United States Army Chaplaincy 1865–1920* (Washington, D.C.: Office of the Chief of Chaplains, 1977), 204; and Robert L. Gushwa, *The Best and Worst of Times. The United States Army Chaplaincy 1920–1945* (Washington, D.C.: Office of the Chief of Chaplains, 1977), 97.

2. See the recent survey by Baylor University: *American Piety in the 21st Century: New Insights to the Depth and Complexity of Religion in the US*, Baylor Institute for Studies of Religion (Waco: Baylor University, September 2006) 8. <www.baylor.edu/content/services/documents.php/3304.pdf>.

3. As an example of some of these ideas shared by the Christian groups see the 1963 Baptist Faith and Mission Statement in W. L. Lumpkin, *Baptist Confessions of Faith*, rev. ed. (Valley Forge, PA: Judson, 1969) 393–400. All three of the groups, Jewish, *Protestant, and Catholic, would agree: The "Bible," at least in part, is authoritative for faith; there is only one God, the God of the Bible; God reigns over the universe with providential care; God created human beings in his image; God will bring the world to its appropriate end in his own time.

4. 1986 *Southern Baptist Convention Bulletin*, 12, col. 2. See Charles W. Hedrick, "Dancing a Little Sidestep: The Southern Baptist Peace Committee Report," *Perspectives in Religious Studies* 15.1 (1988) 25–36.

5. See Jackson W. Carroll, Douglas W. Johnson, Martin E. Marty, and George Gallup Jr., *Religion in America: 1950 to the Present* (New York: Harper & Row, 1979) 28–35, 116–18; George Gallup Jr., *Religion in America,* 1984 (Princeton: Princeton Religion Research

Notes

Center, 1984) 69–77; Martin Marty, Stuart E. Rosenberg, and Andrew M. Greeley, *What Do We Believe? The Stance of Religion in America* (New York: Meredith, 1968) 164–342. *American Piety in the 21st Century*, 30; Rodney Stark, *What Americans Really Believe* (Waco, TX: Baylor University Press, 2008).

Chapter 1

1. Using a masculine pronoun to refer to God is simply a convenience necessitated by the weakness of the English language; God has no gender.

Chapter 3

1. Carl Mirra, "George W. Bush's Theological Diplomacy" on AmericanDiplomacy.org (October 15, 2003) <http://www.unc.edu/depts/diplomat/archives_roll/2003_10-12/mirra_theol/mirra_theol.ntml>.

Chapter 8

1. H. L. Mencken, *Treatise on the Gods* (New York: Random House, 1930) 235–36.
2. See Charles W. Hedrick, "The 'Good News' about the Historical Jesus," in *The Historical Jesus Goes to Church* (Santa Rosa, CA: Polebridge, 2004) 91–103.
3. Charles W. Hedrick, "Out of the Enchanted Forest: Christian Faith in an Age of Reason," in *When Faith Meets Reason*, 13–24.

GLOSSARY

(Brief definitions of the words in the text marked by a star)

Abelard, Peter: A medieval philosopher, academic, and theologian tried for heresy at the Council of Sens in 1140. His ideas were condemned as heretical; he was placed under a ban of perpetual silence and his writings condemned.

Abraham: The traditional founder of the Hebrew people and their descendants; see Genesis 12:1–3. Abraham, *Isaac, and *Jacob are patriarchs of Hebrew faith and are cited together to evoke the authority of the Hebrew tradition; see for example, Exodus 3:6; Mark 12:26; and Acts 3:13.

Abu Ghraib: An American prison in Iraq operated by American soldiers for Iraqi prisoners of war during the administration of George W. Bush.

Achilles: The greatest of Greek heroes and the main character in *Homer's Iliad. He is the son of Peleus, a mortal who was the king of Aegina (a Greek island) and Thetis, a sea nymph, who was a Greek Goddess.

Aegean Sea: The sea between Greece and Asia Minor. The Greeks derived its name from Aegeus, the father of Theseus, a legendary king of Athens.

Agamemnon: King of Mycene, and the leader of the Greek contingent against Troy, a walled city in northwest Asia Minor near the Hellespont, described in *Homer's Illiad.

Ahkenaten: An Egyptian Pharaoh, the husband of Nefertiti, who in the fourteenth century B.C.E. moved the capital from Thebes to Amarna, and began worshipping *Aten (the sun). The ancient Egyptians were *polytheistic. Ahkenaten worshipped only one God, the Aten.

Alexander the Great: The king of Macedon who in the fourth century B.C.E. united the Greek city-states and expanded his kingdom to the Indus River, amassing the largest empire that had ever existed. He conceived himself as the divine son of *Zeus.

Amalekites: A wandering tribe, descended from Esau (Genesis 36:12); the tribe was a problem to the Israelites on their conquest of *Canaan (Deuteronomy 25:17–19; Exodus 17:8–16).

Aphrodite: An ancient Greek Goddess, whose worship was concerned with sexuality and procreation. She was engendered through the severed genitals of *Uranus.

Apollonius: A first-century *Pythagorean wise man of Tyana, whose career rivaled that of Jesus, according to pagan apologists. At his death he was taken bodily into heaven.

Apollo: A Greek God, the son of *Zeus and Leto, a Greek Goddess (Titan). Among his many concerns were healing, music, and poetry.

Aristotle: A fourth-century B.C.E Greek philosopher, and pupil of Plato.

Asclepius: A demi-god (hero), the son of the Greek God *Apollo and Coronis, the daughter of a king of Thessaly. He was the greatest healing figure of Graeco-Roman antiquity.

Aten: Originally Aten was the sun as a heavenly body and later the visible sun disc, representing the creative force of the Aten, the sun God worshipped by *Ahhenaten.

Attica: A geographical region in southeast Greece around the city of Athens.

Augur: An ancient Roman official charged with observing and interpreting omens for the purpose of guiding the state. The omens, or auspices, were of five types: watching birds, the sky, the sacred chickens, quadrupeds, and unusual occurrences.

Ayatollah Khomeini: The chief Shiite Islamic law scholar and head of state in Iran in the 1980s.

Baʻal: A *Canaanite subordinate deity who gained supremacy in the fourteenth century B.C.E. He was God of rain and fertility.

Brown, John: An abolitionist who tried to force a slave rebellion by attacking the U.S. Armory at Harpers Ferry, Virginia, in 1859. A devout man, he believed himself to be acting with God's leadership.

Buddha: Indian religious leader during the fourth/fifth century B.C.E and the founder of Buddhism.

Canaan: The name the original inhabitants of Syria-*Palestine called their land at the time the ancient Israelites invaded the area (see for example Joshua and Judges).

Canaanites: The original inhabitants of Syria-*Palestine at the time the ancient Israelites invaded the area (see Joshua and Judges). They were *polytheistic and their gods were involved with the cycles of nature. Since 1929 hundreds of Canaanite clay tablets written in cuneiform were discovered at Ras Shamra (ancient Ugarit) on the Syrian coast opposite Cyprus.

Canon: The word means rule or guide and generally refers to a collection of writings in communities of faith having some kind of religious authority. In Christianity, the canon is comprised of thirty-nine books of the Hebrew Bible (in the Protestant Bible, but Roman Catholics have several other books) plus twenty-nine books in the New Testament.

Carlin, George: A recently deceased (2008) American stand-up comedian whose humor is dark, ribald, satirical, and sarcastic.

Celtic religion: The Celts are known principally through physical remains in Britain and Western Europe including northern Italy, France, Belgium, and the southern Netherlands. The ancient Celtic use of mistletoe, which was harvested by the Druid priests, was in connection with the sacrifice of two white bulls. The mistletoe was divided among the people and the sprigs were then placed over the doors of their dwellings because of their supposed curative powers.

A Christmas Carol: A book written by the English novelist Charles Dickens in 1843.

Cicero: Marcus Tullius Cicero, a Roman politician, lawyer, orator, and prolific writer in Rome in the first century B.C.E. His essay on divination is titled *De Divinatione* ("On Divination").

Constantine: the Roman general who became emperor in 312 C.E. by his defeat of another contender (Maxentius) near the Milvian Bridge in Italy. Crediting the Christian God with his success, he adopted a conciliatory policy toward the Christian church and extended benefactions to it.

Counter-Reformation: Actually a spiritual renewal movement within the Catholic Church that sought to correct clergy abuses following the *Protestant Reformation.

Cratchit, Bob: A character in *A Christmas Carol*, by Charles Dickens.

Crete: The fifth largest island in the Mediterranean and the largest of the Greek islands. The ancient culture of Crete was called *Minoan.

Cronus: In Greek mythology, the youngest of the divine family of Titans. His marriage to his sister Rhea produced the divine family of the *Olympian deities, of whom *Zeus was the chief God.

Cyclades: A group of Greek Islands in the *Aegean Sea.

Darwin, Charles: An early nineteenth-century naturalist and author, whose book *The Origin of the Species* (1859), established a solid basis for the theory of the evolution of life forms through natural selection of those best adapted to survive.

Descartes, René: An early seventeenth-century French philosopher and mathematician. In his *Discourse on Method* (1637) he set out to establish a solid basis for knowledge through human reason. Doubting all knowledge and philosophical theories, he finally concluded "I think; therefore I exist," and proceeded through careful rational deduction to argue for the existence of human beings, the world, and God.

Deutero-canonical: Ancient Jewish writings taken out of the *Protestant Old Testament because they were not in the Hebrew Scriptures. Roman Catholics affirmed them at the Council of Trent in 1546 as authoritative as the *Proto-canonical books. For Roman Catholics the word means they were added to the *canon at a later time.

Delphi: In ancient Greece, a religious sanctuary of the Greek God *Apollo on the slopes of Mt. Parnassus; it was one of four major sanctuaries that attracted worshippers from all over Greece. The counsel of the Delphian *Oracle was sought by many throughout the ancient world.

Dionysus: The son of *Zeus, who disguised as a mortal, had a love affair with Semele, the mortal daughter of the king of Thebes. He eventually replaced Hestia, Zeus's sister, among the twelve *Olympian gods. He was chiefly known as the god of wine and intoxication.

Eden: The mythical garden in the Hebrew Bible where *Yahweh created the first man and woman. There are two accounts of creation: Genesis 1:1—2:4a and Genesis 2:4b—3:24. Eden is part of the second narrative but not the first.

Elysian Fields: In ancient Greek tradition it was originally a paradise for the distinguished dead, and later it became the abode of the "good" after their deaths.

Enlightenment: An eighteenth-century philosophical and scientific movement in Europe and America that gave birth to the critical method, the rejection of the hegemony of Christian belief, and the rise of reliance on human reason.

ENRON: An American corporation (natural gas pipeline) that was forced to declare bankruptcy after the public disclosure of irregular accounting procedures bordering on fraud.

Epiphany: In general, a great demonstration or manifestation of any divine power. In a narrow sense, it refers to the celebration on January 6 of Jesus' manifestation to Israel as the son of God at his baptism. It was later extended to celebrate the birth of Jesus, including the visit of the magi, and Jesus' childhood events up to the baptism.

Fundamentalism: A movement arising in early twentieth-century *Protestantism that stresses the Bible as the infallible, literal Word of God, absolutely authoritative in matters of faith and doctrine. For example, Adam and Eve were real persons and the world was created in six twenty-four hour days.

Gnostic: The term means "knower." The term describes a series of movements around the time of the emergence of Christianity. In general Gnosticism, in its Christian and Jewish versions, understood creation to be a negative act by the creator God of the Hebrew Bible, whom they rejected as flawed.

Great Mother Goddess: A Goddess of the *Minoan Bronze Age (around 3500–1100 B.C.E.). Her rites were associated with nature, the earth, and fertility. The explanation of the nature of the Goddess is not based on texts but on the interpretation of wall paintings from the period.

Greek Orthodox Church: *Orthodoxy is an ancient eastern Christian movement that has been distinguished since the fifth century from its western version, preserved initially by the Roman Catholic Church and later the churches of the *Protestant Reformation in the west. It is known by its state designations; for example, the Orthodox Church in Greece is the state church of Greece.

Gump, Forrest: A fictional character in a film by the same name released in 1994. The Forest Gump character is portrayed as a mentally challenged man who achieves in spite of his handicap.

Hellas: The name by which the ancient Greeks called their homeland. The inhabitants of this ancient land referred to themselves as Hellenes, and the modern Greeks still do.

Hellenistic: A term applied to the culture that followed *Alexander's conquest of the Mediterranean basin. Alexander had intended to bring classical Greek culture (Hellenic) to the peoples he conquered, but the cultural initiatives he brought to the conquered peoples blended with the indigenous culture to produce a hybrid Greek culture (Hellenistic), enduring from 323 B.C.E. (Alexander) to 410 C.E. (the disintegration of the *Roman Empire).

Hercules: A Greek hero known for his great physical prowess and epic deeds. He was a demi-God whose mother was a human (Alcmene) and his father was the God *Zeus.

Hindu: A devotee of Hinduism, an ancient religion in modern India, approximately four thousand years old.

Homer: An eighth-century B.C.E. Greek poet who is credited with writing the *Iliad*, an epic poem describing the tenth year in the Greek siege of the ancient city of Troy in northwest Asia Minor, and the *Odyssey*, an epic poem describing the return home of the hero Odysseus after the siege of Troy.

Hubris: Arrogance or excessive pride.

Invincible Sun: In 274 C.E. the Roman Emperor Aurelian made the worship of *sol invictus* (the Invincible Sun) the imperial religion of Rome (appealing largely to the advantaged classes). His birthday was celebrated on December 25 (as was that of *Mithras) at the conclusion of his festival, the *Saturnalia. The last non-Christian emperor, Julian (361–363),

Glossary

used the worship of the sun in an attempt to reestablish paganism in the empire.

Ionia: A geographical region on the west cost of Asia Minor, which included the islands off the coast settled by the ancient Greeks.

Isaac: The son of *Abraham and Sarah and the father of *Jacob and Esau; see Genesis 21:1-4.

Isis: An ancient Egyptian goddess of fertility who emerged in the *Hellenistic period as the deity of a mystery cult. She was worshipped as the one and only deity, whom others knew by different names and rites. She promised to fill the deepest needs of her initiates in this world and the next.

Jacob: The second son of Isaac and Rebekah; see Genesis 25:19-26.

Jones, Jim: The founder of the Peoples Temple, an independent church out of the mainstream.

Jonestown: A community founded in 1977 by *Jim Jones in Guyana for the Peoples Temple members. It was intended to be a utopian agricultural community. After a U.S. Congressman and others in his party were killed during a Jonestown visit in 1978, nine hundred eighty members of the Temple died by shooting, poisoned beverage, or forced cyanide injections.

Kismet: Fate or destiny.

Leonidas: A *Spartan general who led three hundred Spartan soldiers and others to delay the advance of an overwhelming Persian force at *Thermopylae in northern Greece in 480 B.C.E. A much larger Greek force met and defeated the Persians later in a sea battle at Artemesium in southern Greece.

Libyan Sea: The Mediterranean Sea between the southern Cretan coast and the coast of Libya.

Luther, Martin: A German theologian and author, and a leading figure of the *Protestant Reformation in the sixteenth century. He was first to translate the Bible into a modern European language (German) directly from the Hebrew and Greek.

Magus: An astrologer, wizard, or sorcerer. It is the Greek word the Gospel of Matthew uses to describe the visitors from the east who came to pay homage to Jesus (Matthew 2:1-12).

Menorah: A general term for "lampstand" in Hebrew, but as used in the Hebrew Bible it refers to the seven-branched lampstand of the tabernacle (Exodus 25:31–40), in the Second Temple (Zechariah 4), and likely in Solomon's temple (1 Kings 7:49) as well. The seven-branched Menorah is used at the time of the Jewish festival of Hanukkah, which occurs in the Jewish calendar around the time of Christmas in the Christian liturgical calendar.

Middle Ages: A period of time roughly between the end of the classical period (around the fifth century C.E.) in European history and the beginning of the Italian *Renaissance (around the fourteenth century).

Milky Way: A vast expanse of innumerable stars stretching across the night sky. It is one of many galaxies in the universe and is the home of our solar system comprised of earth, sun, and planets.

Minoan: The culture of ancient *Crete in the Bronze Age.

Mithras: Or Mithra; the ancient Persian God of light who emerged in the *Hellenistic period as a Mystery Religions deity. The cult is known from its archeological remains of over four hundred sites and statuary. The best known is the statue of Mithras slaying the bull, a statue whose symbolism relates to the salvation of the individual. Mithraism took advantage of the general worship of the *Invincible Sun late in the third century C.E. by regarding Mithras as a personal object of devotion.

Monad: From a Greek word meaning one, or a single unit.

Muhammad: The Prophet of God (Allah) and the founder of Islam. He is credited with writing the *Qur'an.

Muslim: An adherent of Islam.

National Socialism: The principles and practices of the Nazi Party in Germany in the 1920s to 1940s.

Nirvana: In *Buddhism, a perfect state of mind that brings an infinite transcendental happiness, free of the cravings and distractions of human life.

Octopodi: Transliteration of the Greek word for Octopus. In Greek, literally "eight feet."

O'Hara, Scarlet: The main female character in the novel, *Gone with the Wind* (1936), by Margaret Mitchell.

Olympian gods: The family of gods worshipped in Greece after the Titans. They were: *Aphrodite, *Apollo, Ares, Artemis, Athena, Demeter, Dionysus, Hephaestus, Hera, Hermes, *Poseiden, *Zeus. These are the twelve listed on the Parthenon frieze; there were local variations of the list, however.

Oracles: An oracle was a divine utterance of a God through a priest or priestess in response to a question. Those through whom the God spoke were also called oracles, for example, the oracle of the *Delphian *Apollo.

Orthodox: The term means "right thinking." As a general term it is used to describe the way one particular religious group describes itself and its theological ideas. It also characterizes one branch of fifth-century Christians in the east (see *Greek Orthodox Church). It also is a self-designation of that group in western Christianity forming a *canon of Holy Scripture.

Palestine: On the coastal plain of the modern state of Israel from about 1200 B.C.E. dwelled a people called the Philistines, the enemies of ancient Israel. The coastal plain, their homeland, was called Philistia. The term "Palestine" is derived from the name of this ancient people. The early chief centers of Israelite population were found in the hill country.

Paradise: A place of ideal existence. In *Muslim teaching, Paradise is described in the *Qur'an as a Garden of everlasting bliss, where those who keep faith with God will abide forever.

Pastoral Epistles: The New Testament books of First Timothy, Second Timothy, and Titus.

Pentecost: An ancient Israelite harvest festival coming fifty days after Passover. After the destruction of the Jerusalem temple in 70 C.E., Judaism celebrated it as the giving of the law to Moses. The early Church celebrated it as the moment when the Holy Spirit was given to the church (Acts 2:1–13).

Persian Empire: A large middle eastern empire in the sixth and fifth centuries B.C.E., extending from India to Egypt to Thrace but ending at the coast of Greece in the west.

Piñata: A paper-mâché figure filled with candy and toys and suspended from above at Christmas and birthday parties. Blindfolded children try to break it with sticks.

Polytheism: A belief in many Gods.

Pliny: A first-century Roman author and political figure; Gaius Plinius Secundus called "the Elder," to distinguish him from his equally famous nephew who was also called Pliny.

Poseidon: One of the twelve *Olympian family of gods in ancient Greece. He was the god of the sea, earthquakes, and horses.

Protestant Reformation: A general revolt against abuses, such as the sale of indulgences, in the Roman Catholic Church in the sixteenth century. It began in Germany with *Martin Luther, simultaneously spread throughout Europe, resulting in the establishment of churches that no longer accepted the authority of the Roman Catholic Pope.

Proto-canonical: A term used in Roman Catholicism to distinguish the earliest books in their Old Testament from books added later, which were referred to as *deutero-canonical.

Pythagoras: A sixth-century Greek philosopher and mathematician.

Qur'an: The sacred writings of Islam, believed to have been dictated to God's Prophet, *Muhammed, by the angel Gabriel; it is absolutely binding on *Muslims in matters of religion, law, culture, and politics.

Renaissance: A revival of interest in the classical learning of ancient Greece and Rome spreading across Europe in the fourteenth through the seventeenth centuries.

Roman Empire: The rule of the city of Rome in the Mediterranean basin beginning with the accession of Caesar Augustus (Octavian) to the throne in 31 B.C.E. (at Actium) and enduring until 410 C.E., when Rome was plundered by the Visigoths from northern Europe. The empire extended from Britain and Spain in the west, the coast of Africa and Egypt in the south, Gaul and Germany in the north, and Mesopotamia in the east. The Empire enjoyed an enduring peace (*pax romana*) bringing order and stability to the Roman provinces.

Saddam Hussein: The Dictator of Iraq from 1979 to 2003, when he was deposed by American-led forces.

Saturn: An ancient Roman God of agriculture, civilization, and time. The Romans identified him with *Cronus. Because *Saturnalia was celebrated as his festival, it has been suggested that his function was liberation. The statue of the God was bound through the year and loosed on *Saturnalia.

Saturnalia: A Roman festival held December 17–23. Public offices were closed, banquets were held, and gifts were exchanged. The festival was characterized by merriment, gaiety, and revelry, and for one day slaves were served by their masters.

Septuagint: The Greek translation of the Hebrew Bible containing some books not in the Hebrew Bible. The first five books of the Hebrew Bible were translated into Greek as early as the third century B.C.E. The writers of the New Testament used the Greek version of the Bible and not the Hebrew.

Shangri-la: A fictional utopia located in the Himalayas, invented by James Hilton in the novel *Lost Horizon* (1933).

Solstice: In the summer solstice (around June 21) the days grow shorter and in the winter solstice (around December 22) the days begin to lengthen; hence, the celebration of the solstice as the birth of the sun.

Sparta: An ancient Greek city-state located in the southern part of Greece in the Peloponnese. The culture of the city is known for its strict discipline in the training of soldiers from their youth.

Stevens, Wallace: A major American poet of the twentieth-century; he has been described as a "poet of reality," who describes "things as they are."

Tacitus: A first-century Roman historian and provincial governor.

Thermopylae: The name means "hot gates," for the warm springs in the strategic pass providing the main north-south land route into central and southern Greece.

Tilton, Robert: An American television evangelist who gained notoriety in the 1980s and early 1990s.

Trinity: The explanation of the nature of God, who is conceived as three independent persons in One: Father, Son, and Holy Spirit. The concept emerges in the second century and achieves creedal status in the fourth century.

Tsunami: The Japanese word for a tidal wave caused by earthquake or volcanic action under the sea.

Tyche: Luck, fortune, or chance; in the *Hellenistic period she was personified as a capricious deity and even had a cult devoted to her worship.

Tyndale, William: An Englishman, a man of letters, who in the early sixteenth century was first to translate the Pentateuch from Hebrew into English, and the New Testament from Greek into English. For this endeavor he was burned at the stake in 1536.

Unicorn: Regarded today as a legendary or mythical animal. It resembled a horse and had a single horn in its forehead.

Uranus: In Hesiod's *Theogony*, Uranus is the personification of the sky produced by his mother earth (Gaia). He becomes her consort and they produce divine children. He is the father of *Aphrodite and *Cronus, who later emasculated Uranus.

Vulgate: The Latin translation of the Bible generally credited to Jerome in the fourth century C.E.; so-called because it rendered the Bible into the vernacular ("vulgar" tongue) from Hebrew and Greek.

William Jewell College: A private four-year liberal arts college located in Liberty, Missouri, north of Kansas City. It had historical ties to the Missouri Southern Baptist Convention, but severed connections in 2003 over issues related to evolution and homosexuality.

Wassail bowl: "Wassail!" is an Anglo-Saxon expression offered when drinking to a person's health from a bowl of hot spiced ale and toasted apples.

Yahweh: The personal name of the God of the ancient Israelites. There are several versions of the name because ancient Israelites had no vowels making it subject to different renderings. Another common rendering is Jehovah.

Yule log: Yule is the ordinary name for Christmas in the Scandinavian languages. The Yule log was a large log of wood burned during the twelve days of Christmas. Its charcoal was thought to have certain magical properties.

Zeus: The chief god of the twelve *Olympian deities; he was the son of the Titan god *Cronus and his sister Rhea.

SELECTED BIBLIOGRAPHY

The works in this bibliography are for the general reader not the special-ist. The texts listed here are, where possible, introductory in nature and provide a survey of the issues raised by reason particularly with regard to matters of religious faith.

Brockman, John, editor. *The New Humanists: Science at the Edge*. New York: Barnes & Noble, 2003.

Ehrman, Bart D. *The Orthodox Corruption of Scripture: The Effect of Early Christological Controversies on the Text of the New Testament*. Oxford: Oxford University Press, 1993.

Epp, Eldon Jay, and George MacRae, editors. *The New Testament and Its Modern Inter-preters*. Atlanta: Scholars, 1989.

Ferguson, Everett. *Backgrounds of Early Christianity*. 3rd ed. Grand Rapids: Eerdmans, 2003.

Funk, Robert W. *The Acts of Jesus: The Search for the Authentic Deeds of Jesus*. San Francisco: Harper, 1998.

Funk, Robert W., and Roy W. Hoover. *The Five Gospels: What Did Jesus Really Say?* San Francisco: Harper, 1993.

Gay, Peter, editor. *The Enlightenment: A Comprehensive Anthology*. New York: Simon & Schuster, 1973.

Hahn, Herbert F. *The Old Testament in Modern Research*. Philadelphia: Fortress, 1966.

Harris, Stephen L. *The New Testament: A Student's Introduction*. 5th ed. Boston: McGraw-Hill, 2005.

Bibliography

Hedrick, Charles W. "Miracles in Mark: A Study in Markan Theology and Its Implications for Modern Religious Thought." *Perspectives in Religious Studies* 34.3 (2007) 297–313.

———, editor. *When Faith Meets Reaston. Religion Scholars Reflect on Their Spiritual Journeys*. Santa Rosa, CA: Polebridge, 2008.

Hobson, Christine. *The World of the Pharaohs*. New York: Thames & Hudson, 1987.

Hornblower, Simon, and Antony Spawforth, editors. *The Oxford Classical Dictionary*. 3rd ed. Oxford: Oxford University Press, 1996.

Jeanrond, Werner G. "History of Interpretation [of the Bible]." In *The Anchor Bible Dictionary*, edited by David Noel Freedman, 3:424–43. New York: Doubleday, 1992.

Kuntz, J. Kenneth. *The People of Ancient Israel: An Introduction to Old Testament Literature, History and Thought*. New York: Harper & Row, 1974.

Lerner, Robert E., Standish Meacham, and Edward McNall Burns. *Western Civilizations: Their History and Their Culture*. 13th ed. New York: Norton. 1998.

Mates, Julian, and Eugene Cantelupe, editors. *Renaissance Culture: A New Sense of Order*. New York: Braziller, 1966.

Mazzeo, George Anthony. *Renaissance and Revolution: Remaking of European Thought*. New York: Pantheon, 1965.

Mencken, H. L. *Treatise on the Gods*. New York: Random House, 1930.

Meyer, Marvin, and Richard Smith, editors. *Ancient Christian Magic: Coptic Texts of Ritual Power*. San Francisco: HarperSanFrancisco, 1994.

Miles, Clement A. *Christmas Customs and Traditions: Their History and Significance*. New York: Dover, 1976.

Miller, Robert J. *Born Divine: The Births of Jesus & Other Sons of God*. Santa Rosa, CA: Polebridge, 2003.

Polka, Brayton, and Bernard Zelechow, editors. *Readings in Western Civilization*. 2 vols. New York: Knopf, 1970.

Randall, John Herbert Jr. *The Making of the Modern Mind: A Survey of the Intellectual Background of the Present Age*. Boston: Houghton Mifflin, 1926.

Robinson, John A. T. *Honest to God*. Philadelphia: Westminster, 1963.

Schweitzer, Albert. *The Quest of the Historical Jesus*. Translated by W. Montgomery. New York: Macmillan, 1971.

Rodney Stark, *What Americans Really Believe*. Waco, TX: Baylor University Press, 2008.

Weaver, Walter P. *The Historical Jesus in the Twentieth Century*, 1900–1950. Harrisburg, PA: Trinity, 1999.

Young, Louise B., editor. *Exploring the Universe*. New York: Oxford University Press, 1971.

www.ingramcontent.com/pod-product-compliance
Lightning Source LLC
Chambersburg PA
CBHW020207090426
42734CB00008B/967